John Berger

Why Look at Animals?

PENGUIN BOOKS — GREAT IDEAS

PENGUIN BOOKS

Published by the Penguin Group
Penguin Books Ltd, 80 Strand, London WC2R 0RL, England
Penguin Group (USA) Inc., 375 Hudson Street, New York, New York 10014, USA
Penguin Group (Canada), 90 Eglinton Avenue East, Suite 700, Toronto, Ontario, Canada M4P 2Y3
(a division of Pearson Penguin Canada Inc.)
Penguin Ireland, 25 St Stephen's Green, Dublin 2, Ireland
(a division of Penguin Books Ltd)
Penguin Group (Australia), 250 Camberwell Road, Camberwell, Victoria 3124, Australia
(a division of Pearson Australia Group Pty Ltd)
Penguin Books India Pvt Ltd, 11 Community Centre, Panchsheel Park, New Delhi – 110 017, India
Penguin Group (NZ), 67 Apollo Drive, Rosedale, North Shore 0632, New Zealand
(a division of Pearson New Zealand Ltd)
Penguin Books (South Africa) (Pty) Ltd, 24 Sturdee Avenue,
Rosebank, Johannesburg 2196, South Africa

Penguin Books Ltd, Registered Offices: 80 Strand, London WC2R 0RL, England

www.penguin.com

This selection first published in Penguin Books 2009

007

Set by Rowland Phototypesetting Ltd, Bury St Edmunds, Suffolk
Printed in England by Clays Ltd, St Ives plc

978-0-141-04397-5

www.greenpenguin.co.uk

Contents

Why Look at Animals?

A Mouse Story

Once there was a man who, every morning, picked up a bread-knife and cut off ten centimetres from the loaf of bread he was holding, and threw this chunk away, before cutting another slice for his own breakfast.

The man did this because every night mice had nibbled a hole from the centre of the loaf. Each morning the hole was about the size of a mouse. The house cats, although they hunted moles, were strangely indifferent to the gray mice who ate the bread, or perhaps they had been bought off.

This had been the state of affairs for months. Many times the man had written down *mousetrap* on a shopping list. And many times he had forgotten, perhaps because the shop where the villagers once bought mousetraps no longer existed.

One afternoon this man is searching in a shed beside the house for a metal file. He doesn't find a file, but he comes upon a strong, obviously handmade, mousetrap. It consists of a plank of wood, 18 cm × 9 cm, with a cage around it made of stout wire. The space between any two parallel wires is never more than ½ cm. Enough for a mouse to poke its nose through but never enough to get its two ears through. The height of the cage is 8.5 cm, so that, inside, a mouse can stand up on its strong hind legs, clutch the bars at the top with its four-fingered hands, and poke its snout between the wires of the ceiling, but it can never get out.

One end of the cage is a door which hinges upwards. A spiral spring is attached to this door. When the door is held open, the spring goes taut, ready to pull it back shut. On top of the cage is a trip wire which fastens the door when open. The trip wire, however, extends beyond the doorframe by less than a millimetre. In wire-terms by a hair's breadth! At the other end of the wire, inside the cage, is a hook on to which a piece of cheese or raw liver is fixed.

The mouse enters the cage to take a bite. No sooner does he touch the morsel with his teeth, than the trip wire releases the door and it slams shut behind him, before he can turn his head.

It takes the mouse several hours to realize that he is a prisoner, unhurt, in a cage measuring 18 cm by 9 cm. After that, something in him never stops trembling.

The man takes the mousetrap into the house. He tests it. He fixes a lump of cheese on to the hook and places the trap on the shelf in the cupboard where the bread is kept.

Next morning the man finds a gray mouse in the cage. The cheese in the cage is untouched. Since the door was shut, the mouse lost his appetite. When the man picks up the cage, the mouse tries to hide behind the spring attached to the door. The mouse has jet black eyes which stare without blinking. The man places the cage on the kitchen table. The longer he looks into the cage, the more clearly he sees a resemblance between the sitting mouse and a kangaroo. There is a silence. The mouse becomes a little calmer. Then the mouse begins to circle the cage, testing again and again with one of his fingered fore paws the space between the wires, searching for an exception. The mouse tries biting the wires with his teeth. Then he sits back on his haunches, paws to his mouth. Rarely does somebody look at a mouse as long as the man does. Or visa versa.

The man takes the cage to a field outside the village, places it on the grass and opens the door. It takes the mouse a minute to realize the fourth wall has disappeared. He tests the open space with his muzzle. Then he darts out, and scuttles to the nearest tuft of grass where he hides.

The next day the man finds another mouse in the cage. He's heavier than the first, but more agitated. Perhaps he is older. The man puts the cage on the floor and sits on the floor himself to watch. The mouse climbs on to the wires of the ceiling and holds himself there upside down. When the man opens the cage in the field, the old mouse runs away in a zig-zag line until he's out of sight.

One morning the man finds two mice in the cage. It's hard to say how much they are aware of each other, or to guess whether the presence of the other lessens or increases their mutual fear. One has larger ears, the other glossier hair. Mice resemble kangaroos because of the relatively enormous force of their hind legs, and the way their strong tails press against the ground for leverage when they leap.

In the field, when the man lifts the fourth wall, the two mice do not hesitate. They leave immediately, side by side, and take opposite directions, one going east and the other west.

Scarcely any bread in the cupboard has been eaten. The mouse, when the man picks up the cage, reacts with the usual panic, but moves more heavily. The man leaves the kitchen to take his mail and to chat for a moment with the postman. When he returns, there are nine newly born mice in the cage. Perfectly formed. Pink. Each one twice the size of a grain of long rice.

After ten days, the man asks himself whether some of the mice he has released in the field are not returning to the house. He decides, on reflection, that this is unlikely. He observes each one so closely that he is convinced that, should one return, he would have recognized her or him immediately.

The mouse in the cage holds his head on one side as if he was wearing a cap. His two front paws, with their four fingers, are planted firmly on the ground either side of his muzzle, like the hands of a pianist on a keyboard. His hind legs are tucked in close and extend along the ground so that they are almost under his ears. His ears are perked up, and his tail, stretched out far behind him, is pressed firmly on the floor of the cage. His heart's beating very fast and he is frightened when the man lifts up the cage. Yet he doesn't hide behind the spring; he doesn't cringe. He holds his head acock, and he stares back. For the first time, a name for the mouse comes in to the man's head. Alfredo, he calls him. He puts the cage on the kitchen table beside his coffee cup.

Later the man goes to the field, kneels down, places the cage on the grass and holds the door, which is the fourth wall of the cell, open. The mouse approaches the open wall, raises his head, and leaps. He does not scuttle, he does not dart, he flies. Relative to his size, he leaps higher and further than a kangaroo. He leaps like a mouse who has been freed. With three leaps he has covered more than five metres. And the man, still on his knees, watches the mouse he called Alfredo leap again and again into the sky.

The following morning the bread has not been touched. And the man believes the mouse in the cage may be the last one. Kneeling in the field outside the village, holding the door open, the man waits. It takes the mouse a long while to realize he can leave. When he finally does, he scuttles into the thickest and nearest tuft of grass, and the man feels a slight yet sharp pang of disappointment. He had been hoping to see, one more time in his life, a prisoner fly, a prisoner realize his dream of freedom.

2009

Opening a Gate

The ceiling of the bedroom is painted a faded sky blue. There are two large rusty hooks screwed into the beams and from these, long ago, the farmer hung his smoked sausages and hams. This is the room in which I'm writing. Outside the window are old plum trees, the fruit now turning raven blue, and beyond them the nearest hill which forms the first step to the mountains.

Early this morning, when I was still in bed, a swallow flew in, circled the room, saw its error and flew out through the window past the plum trees to alight on the telephone wire. I relate this small incident because it seems to me to have something to do with Pentti Sammallahti's photographs. They too, like the swallow, are aberrant.

I have had some of his photographs in the house now for two years. I often take them out of their folder to show to friends who pass. They usually gasp at first, and then peer closer, smiling. They look at the places shown for a longer time than is usual with a photograph. Perhaps they ask whether I know the photographer, Pentti Sammallahti, personally? Or they ask what part of Russia were they taken in? In what year? They never try to put their evident pleasure into words, for it is a secret one. They simply look closer and remember. What?

In each of these pictures there is at least one dog. That's clear and it might be no more than a gimmick. Yet in fact the dogs offer a key for opening a door. No, a gate – for here everything is outside, outside and beyond.

I notice also in each photograph the special light, the light determined by the time of day or the season of the year. It is, invariably, the light in which figures hunt – for animals, forgotten names, a path leading home, a new day, sleep, the next lorry, spring. A light in which there is no permanence, a light of nothing longer than a glimpse. This too is a key to opening the gate.

The photos were taken with a panoramic camera, such as is normally used for making wide-section geological surveys. Here the wide-section is important, not, I think, for aesthetic reasons but, once again, for scientific, observational ones. A lens with a narrower focus would not have found what I now see, and so it would have remained invisible. What do I now see?

We live our daily lives in a constant exchange with the set of daily appearances surrounding us – often they are very familiar, sometimes they are unexpected and new, but always they confirm us in our lives. They do so even when they are threatening: the sight of a house burning, for example, or a man approaching us with a knife between his teeth, still reminds us (urgently) of our life and its importance. What we habitually see confirms us.

Yet it can happen, suddenly, unexpectedly, and most frequently in the half-light-of-glimpses, that we catch sight of another visible order which intersects with ours and has nothing to do with it.

The speed of a cinema film is 25 frames per second. God knows how many frames per second flicker past in our daily perception. But it is as if, at the brief moments I'm talking about, suddenly and disconcertingly we see *between* two frames. We come upon a part of the visible which wasn't destined for us. Perhaps it was destined for night-birds, reindeer, ferrets, eels, whales . . .

Our customary visible order is not the only one: it coexists with other orders. Stories of fairies, sprites, ogres were a human attempt to come to terms with this coexistence. Hunters are continually aware of it and so can read signs we do not see. Children feel it intuitively, because they have the habit of hiding behind things. There they discover the interstices between different sets of the visible.

Dogs, with their running legs, sharp noses and developed memory for sounds, are the natural frontier experts of these interstices. Their eyes, whose message often confuses us for it is urgent and mute, are attuned both to the human order and to other visible orders. Perhaps this is why, on so many occasions and for different reasons, we train dogs as guides.

Probably it was a dog who led the great Finnish photographer to the moment and place for the taking of these pictures. In each one the human order, still in sight, is nevertheless no longer central and is slipping away. The interstices are open.

The result is unsettling: there is more solitude, more pain, more dereliction. At the same time, there is an expectancy which I have not experienced since childhood, since I talked to dogs, listened to their secrets and kept them to myself.

2001

Why Look at Animals?

For Gilles Aillaud

The 19th century, in western Europe and North America, saw the beginning of a process, today being completed by 20th-century corporate capitalism, by which every tradition which has previously mediated between man and nature was broken. Before this rupture, animals constituted the first circle of what surrounded man. Perhaps that already suggests too great a distance. They were with man at the centre of his world. Such centrality was of course economic and productive. Whatever the changes in productive means and social organization, men depended upon animals for food, work, transport, clothing.

Yet to suppose that animals first entered the human imagination as meat or leather or horn is to project a 19th-century attitude backwards across the millennia. Animals first entered the imagination as messengers and promises. For example, the domestication of cattle did not begin as a simple prospect of milk and meat. Cattle had magical functions, sometimes oracular, sometimes sacrificial. And the choice of a given species as magical, tameable *and* alimentary was originally determined by the habits, proximity and 'invitation' of the animal in question.

White ox good is my mother
And we the people of my sister,
The people of Nyariau Bul . . .
Friend, great ox of the spreading horns,
which ever bellows amid the herd,
Ox of the son of Bul Maloa.

(*The Nuer: a description of the modes of livelihood and political
institutions of a Nilotic people*, by Evans-Pritchard.)

Animals are born, are sentient and are mortal. In these
things they resemble man. In their superficial anatomy
– less in their deep anatomy – in their habits, in their
time, in their physical capacities, they differ from man.
They are both like and unlike.

'We know what animals do and what beaver and bears and
salmon and other creatures need, because once our men were
married to them and they acquired this knowledge from their
animal wives.' (Hawaiian Indians quoted by Lévi-Strauss in
The Savage Mind.)

The eyes of an animal when they consider a man are
attentive and wary. The same animal may well look at
other species in the same way. He does not reserve a
special look for man. But by no other species except man
will the animal's look be recognized as familiar. Other
animals are held by the look. Man becomes aware of
himself returning the look.

The animal scrutinizes him across a narrow abyss of
non-comprehension. This is why the man can surprise

the animal. Yet the animal – even if domesticated – can also surprise the man. The man too is looking across a similar, but not identical, abyss of non-comprehension. And this is so wherever he looks. He is always looking across ignorance and fear. And so, when he is *being seen* by the animal, he is being seen as his surroundings are seen by him. His recognition of this is what makes the look of the animal familiar. And yet the animal is distinct, and can never be confused with man. Thus, a power is ascribed to the animal, comparable with human power but never coinciding with it. The animal has secrets which, unlike the secrets of caves, mountains, seas, are specifically addressed to man.

The relation may become clearer by comparing the look of an animal with the look of another man. Between two men the two abysses are, in principle, bridged by language. Even if the encounter is hostile and no words are used (even if the two speak different languages), the *existence* of language allows that at least one of them, if not both mutually, is confirmed by the other. Language allows men to reckon with each other as with themselves. (In the confirmation made possible by language, human ignorance and fear may also be confirmed. Whereas in animals fear is a response to signal, in men it is endemic.)

No animal confirms man, either positively or negatively. The animal can be killed and eaten so that its energy is added to that which the hunter already possesses. The animal can be tamed so that it supplies and works for the peasant. But always its lack of common language, its silence, guarantees its distance, its distinctness, its exclusion, from and of man.

Just because of this distinctness, however, an animal's life, never to be confused with a man's, can be seen to run parallel to his. Only in death do the two parallel lines converge and after death, perhaps, cross over to become parallel again: hence the widespread belief in the transmigration of souls.

With their parallel lives, animals offer man a companionship which is different from any offered by human exchange. Different because it is a companionship offered to the loneliness of man as a species.

Such an unspeaking companionship was felt to be so equal that often one finds the conviction that it was man who lacked the capacity to speak with animals – hence the stories and legends of exceptional beings, like Orpheus, who could talk with animals in their own language.

What were the secrets of the animal's likeness with, and unlikeness from, man? The secrets whose existence man recognized as soon as he intercepted an animal's look.

In one sense the whole of anthropology, concerned with the passage from nature to culture, is an answer to that question. But there is also a general answer. All the secrets were about animals as an *intercession* between man and his origin. Darwin's evolutionary theory, indelibly stamped as it is with the marks of the European 19th century, nevertheless belongs to a tradition, almost as old as man himself. Animals interceded between man and their origin because they were both like and unlike man.

Animals came from over the horizon. They belonged

there and *here*. Likewise they were mortal and immortal. An animal's blood flowed like human blood, but its, species was undying and each lion was Lion, each ox was Ox. This – maybe the first existential dualism – was reflected in the treatment of animals. They were subjected *and* worshipped, bred *and* sacrificed.

Today the vestiges of this dualism remain among those who live intimately with, and depend upon, animals. A peasant becomes fond of his pig and is glad to salt away its pork. What is significant, and is so difficult for the urban stranger to understand, is that the two statements in that sentence are connected by an *and* and not by a *but*.

The parallelism of their similar/dissimilar lives allowed animals to provoke some of the first questions and offer answers. The first subject matter for painting was animal. Probably the first paint was animal blood. Prior to that, it is not unreasonable to suppose that the first metaphor was animal. Rousseau, in his *Essay on the Origins of Languages*, maintained that language itself began with metaphor: 'As emotions were the first motives which induced man to speak, his first utterances were tropes (metaphors). Figurative language was the first to be born, proper meanings were the last to be found.'

If the first metaphor was animal, it was because the essential relation between man and animal was metaphoric. Within that relation what the two terms – man and animal – shared in common revealed what differentiated them. And vice versa.

In his book on totemism, Lévi-Strauss comments on

Rousseau's reasoning: 'It is because man originally felt himself identical to all those like him (among which, as Rousseau explicitly says, we must include animals) that he came to acquire the capacity to distinguish *himself* as he distinguishes *them* – ie, to use the diversity of species for conceptual support for social differentiation.'

To accept Rousseau's explanation of the origins of language is, of course, to beg certain questions (what was the minimal social organisation necessary for the breakthrough of language?). Yet no search for origin can ever be fully satisfied. The intercession of animals in that search was so common precisely because animals remain ambiguous.

All theories of ultimate origin are only ways of better defining what followed. Those who disagree with Rousseau are contesting a view of man, not a historical fact. What we are trying to define, because the experience is almost lost, is the universal use of animal-signs for charting the experience of the world.

Animals were seen in eight out of twelve signs of the zodiac. Among the Greeks, the sign of each of the twelve hours of the day was an animal. (The first a cat, the last a crocodile.) The Hindus envisaged the earth being carried on the back of an elephant and the elephant on a tortoise. For the Nuer of the southern Sudan (see Roy Willis's *Man and Beast*), 'all creatures, including man, originally lived together in fellowship in one camp. Dissension began after Fox persuaded Mongoose to throw a club into Elephant's face. A quarrel ensued and the animals separated; each went its own way and began to live as they now are, and to kill each other. Stomach, which at first lived a life of its own in the bush, entered into man so that now he is always hungry. The sexual organs, which had also been separate, attached themselves to men and women, causing them to desire one another constantly. Elephant taught man how to pound millet so that now he satisfies his hunger only by ceaseless labour. Mouse taught man to beget and women to bear. And Dog brought fire to man.'

The examples are endless. Everywhere animals offered explanations, or, more precisely, lent their name or character to a quality, which like all qualities was, in its essence, mysterious.

What distinguished man from animals was the human capacity for symbolic thought, the capacity which was inseparable from the development of language in which words were not mere signals, but signifiers of something other than themselves. Yet the first symbols were animals. What distinguished men from animals was born of their relationship with them.

The *Iliad* is one of the earliest texts available to us, and in it the use of metaphor still reveals the proximity of man and animal, the proximity from which metaphor itself arose. Homer describes the death of a soldier on the battlefield and then the death of a horse. Both deaths are equally transparent to Homer's eyes, there is no more refraction in one case than the other.

'Meanwhile, Idomeneus struck Erymas on the mouth with his relentless bronze. The metal point of the spear passed right through the lower part of his skull, under the brain and smashed the white bones. His teeth were shattered; both his eyes were filled with blood; and he spurted blood through his nostrils and his gaping mouth. Then the black cloud of Death descended on him.' That was a man.

Three pages further on, it is a horse who falls: 'Sarpedon, casting second with his shining spear, missed Patroclus but struck his horse Pedasus on the right shoulder. The horse whinnied in the throes of Death, then fell down in the dust and with a great sigh gave up his life.' That was animal.

Book 17 of the *Iliad* opens with Menelaus standing over the corpse of Patroclus to prevent the Trojans stripping it. Here Homer uses animals as metaphoric references, to convey, with irony or admiration, the excessive or superlative qualities of different moments. *Without the example of animals* such moments would have remained indescribable. 'Menelaus bestrode his body like a fretful mother cow standing over the first calf she has brought into the world.'

A Trojan threatens him, and ironically Menelaus shouts out to Zeus: 'Have you ever seen such arrogance? We know the courage of the panther and the lion and the fierce wild-boar, the most high-spirited and self-reliant beast of all, but that, it seems, is nothing to the prowess of these sons of Panthous . . . !'

Menelaus then kills the Trojan who threatened him, and nobody dares approach him. 'He was like a mountain lion who believes in his own strength and pounces on the finest heifer in a grazing herd. He breaks her neck with his powerful jaws, and then he tears her to pieces and devours her blood and entrails, while all around him the herdsmen and their dogs create a din but keep their distance – they are heartily scared of him and nothing would induce them to close in.'

Centuries after Homer, Aristotle, in his *History of Animals*, the first major scientific work on the subject, systematizes the comparative relation of man and animal.

In the great majority of animals there are traces of physical qualities and attitudes, which qualities are more markedly differentiated in the case of human beings. For just as we pointed out resemblances in the physical organs, so in a number of animals we observe gentleness and fierceness, mildness or cross-temper, courage or timidity, fear or confidence, high spirits or low cunning, and, with regard to intelligence, something akin to sagacity. Some of these qualities in man, as compared with the corresponding qualities in animals, differ only quantitatively: that is to say, man has more or less of this quality, and an animal has more or less of some other; other qualities in man are represented by analogous and not identical qualities; for example, just as in man we find knowledge, wisdom and sagacity, so in certain animals there exists some other natural potentiality akin to these. The truth of this statement will be the more clearly apprehended if we have regard to the phenomena of childhood: for in children we observe the traces and seeds of what will one day be settled psychological habits, though psychologically a child hardly differs for the time being from an animal . . .

To most modern 'educated' readers, this passage, I think, will seem noble but too anthropomorphic. Gentleness, cross-temper, sagacity, they would argue, are not moral qualities which can be ascribed to animals. And the behaviourists would support this objection.

Until the 19th century, however, anthropomorphism was integral to the relation between man and animal and was an expression of their proximity. Anthropomorphism was the residue of the continuous use of animal metaphor. In the last two centuries, animals have gradually disappeared. Today we live without them. And in this new solitude, anthropomorphism makes us doubly uneasy.

The decisive theoretical break came with Descartes. Descartes internalized, *within man*, the dualism implicit in the human relation to animals. In dividing absolutely body from soul, he bequeathed the body to the laws of physics and mechanics, and, since animals were soulless, the animal was reduced to the model of a machine.

The consequences of Descartes's break followed only slowly. A century later, the great zoologist Buffon, although accepting and using the model of the machine in order to classify animals and their capacities, nevertheless displays a tenderness towards animals which temporarily reinstates them as companions. This tenderness is half envious.

What man has to do in order to transcend the animal, to transcend the mechanical within himself, and what his unique spirituality leads to, is often anguish. And so, by comparison and despite the model of the machine, the animal seems to him to enjoy a kind of innocence. The animal has been emptied of experience and secrets, and this new invented 'innocence' begins to provoke in man a kind of nostalgia. For the first time, animals are placed in a *receding* past. Buffon, writing on the beaver, says this:

To the same degree as man has raised himself above the state of nature, animals have fallen below it: conquered and turned into slaves, or treated as rebels and scattered by force, their societies have faded away, their industry has become unproductive, their tentative arts have disappeared; each species has lost its general qualities, all of them retaining only their distinct capacities, developed in some by example, imitation, education, and in others, by fear and necessity during the constant watch for survival. What visions and plans can these soulless slaves have, these relics of the past without power?

Only vestiges of their once marvellous industry remain in far deserted places, unknown to man for centuries, where each species freely used its natural capacities and perfected them in peace within a lasting community. The beavers are perhaps the only remaining example, the last monument to that animal intelligence . . .

Although such nostalgia towards animals was an 18th-century invention, countless *productive* inventions were still necessary – the railway, electricity, the conveyor belt, the canning industry, the motor car, chemical fertilisers – before animals could be marginalized.

During the 20th century, the internal combustion engine displaced draught animals in streets and factories. Cities, growing at an ever increasing rate, transformed the surrounding countryside into suburbs where field animals, wild or domesticated, became rare. The commercial exploitation of certain species (bison, tigers, reindeer) has rendered them almost extinct. Such wild life as remains is increasingly confined to national parks and game reserves.

Eventually, Descartes's model was surpassed. In the first stages of the industrial revolution, animals were used as machines. As also were children. Later, in the so-called post-industrial societies, they are treated as raw material. Animals required for food are processed like manufactured commodities.

Another giant [plant], now under development in North Carolina, will cover a total of 150,000 hectares but will employ only 1,000 people, one for every 15 hectares. Grains will be sown, nurtured and harvested by machines, including airplanes. They will be fed to the 50,000 cattle and hogs . . . those animals will never touch the ground. They will be bred, suckled and fed to maturity in specially designed pens. (Susan George's *How the Other Half Dies*.)

This reduction of the animal, which has a theoretical as well as economic history, is part of the same process as that by which men have been reduced to isolated productive and consuming units. Indeed, during this period an approach to animals often prefigured an approach to man. The mechanical view of the animal's work capacity was later applied to that of workers. F. W. Taylor who developed the 'Taylorism' of time-motion studies and 'scientific' management of industry proposed that work must be 'so stupid' and so phlegmatic that he (the worker) 'more nearly resembles in his mental make-up the ox than any other type'. Nearly all modern techniques of social conditioning were first established with animal experiments. As were also the methods of so-called intelligence testing. Today behaviourists like Skinner imprison the very concept of man within the limits of what they conclude from their artificial tests with animals.

Is there not one way in which animals, instead of disappearing, continue to multiply? Never have there been so many household pets as are to be found today in the cities of the richest countries. In the United States, it is estimated that there are at least forty million dogs, forty million cats, fifteen million cage birds and ten million other pets.

In the past, families of all classes kept domestic animals because they served a useful purpose – guard dogs, hunting dogs, mice-killing cats, and so on. The practice of keeping animals regardless of their usefulness, the keeping, exactly, of *pets* (in the 16th century the word usually referred to a lamb raised by hand) is a modern innovation, and, on the social scale on which it exists today, is unique. It is part of that universal but personal withdrawal into the private small family unit, decorated or furnished with mementoes from the outside world, which is such a distinguishing feature of consumer societies.

The small family living unit lacks space, earth, other animals, seasons, natural temperatures, and so on. The pet is either sterilized or sexually isolated, extremely limited in its exercise, deprived of almost all other animal contact, and fed with artificial foods. This is the material process which lies behind the truism that pets come to resemble their masters or mistresses. They are creatures of their owner's way of life.

Equally important is the way the average owner regards his pet. (Children are, briefly, somewhat different.) The pet *completes* him, offering responses to aspects of his character which would otherwise remain unconfirmed. He can be to his pet what he is not to anybody or anything else. Furthermore, the pet can be conditioned to react as though it, too, recognizes this. The pet offers its owner a mirror to a part that is otherwise never reflected. But, since in this relationship the autonomy of both parties has been lost (the owner has become the-special-man-he-is-only-to-his-pet, and the animal has become dependent on its owner for every physical need), the parallelism of their separate lives has been destroyed.

The cultural marginalization of animals is, of course, a more complex process than their physical marginalization. The animals of the mind cannot be so easily dispersed. Sayings, dreams, games, stories, superstitions, the language itself, recall them. The animals of the mind, instead of being dispersed, have been co-opted into other categories so that the category *animal* has lost its central importance. Mostly they have been co-opted into the *family* and into the *spectacle*.

Those co-opted into the family somewhat resemble pets. But having no physical needs or limitations as pets do, they can be totally transformed into human puppets. The books and drawings of Beatrix Potter are an early example; all the animal productions of the Disney industry are a more recent and extreme one. In such works the pettiness of current social practices is *universalized* by being projected on to the animal kingdom. The following dialogue between Donald Duck and his nephews is eloquent enough.

DONALD: Man, what a day! What a perfect day for fishing, boating, dating or picnicking – only I can't do *any* of these things!

NEPHEW: Why not, Unca Donald? What's holding you back?

DONALD: The Bread of Life boys! As usual, I'm broke and its eons till payday.

NEPHEW: You could take a walk Unca Donald – go bird-watching.

DONALD: (groan!) I may *have to*! But first, I'll wait for the mailman. He may bring something good newswise!

NEPHEW: Like a cheque from an unknown relative in Moneyville?

Their physical features apart, these animals have been absorbed into the so-called silent majority.

The animals transformed into spectacle have disappeared in another way. In the windows of bookshops at Christmas, a third of the volumes on display are animal picture books. Baby owls or giraffes, the camera fixes them in a domain which, although entirely visible to the camera, will never be entered by the spectator. All animals appear like fish seen through the plate glass of an aquarium. The reasons for this are both technical and ideological: Technically the devices used to obtain ever more arresting images – hidden cameras, telescopic lenses, flashlights, remote controls and so on – combine to produce pictures which carry with them numerous indications of their normal *invisibility*. The images exist thanks only to the existence of a technical clairvoyance.

A recent, very well-produced book of animal photographs (*La Fête Sauvage* by Frédéric Rossif) announces in its preface: 'Each of these pictures lasted in real time less than three hundredths of a second, they are far beyond the capacity of the human eye. What we see here is something never before seen, because it is totally invisible.'

In the accompanying ideology, animals are always the observed. The fact that they can observe us has lost all significance. They are the objects of our ever-extending knowledge. What we know about them is an index of our power, and thus an index of what separates us from them. The more we know, the further away they are.

Yet in the same ideology, as Lukacs points out in *History and Class Consciousness*, nature is also a value concept. A value opposed to the social institutions which strip man of his natural essence and imprison him. 'Nature thereby acquires the meaning of what has grown organically, what was not created by man, in contrast to the artificial structures of human civilization. At the same time, it can be understood as that aspect of human inwardness which has remained natural, or at least tends or longs to become natural once more.' According to this view of nature, the life of a wild animal becomes an ideal, an ideal internalized as a feeling surrounding a repressed desire. The image of a wild animal becomes the starting-point of a daydream: a point from which the daydreamer departs with his back turned.

The degree of confusion involved is illustrated by the following news story: 'London housewife Barbara Carter won a "grant a wish" charity contest, and said she wanted to kiss and cuddle a lion. Wednesday night she was in a hospital in shock and with throat wounds. Mrs Carter, 46, was taken to the lions' compound of the safari park at Bewdley, Wednesday. As she bent forward to stroke the lioness, Suki, it pounced and dragged her to the ground. Wardens later said, "We seem to have made a bad error of judgment. We have always regarded the lioness as perfectly safe."'

The treatment of animals in 19th-century romantic painting was already an acknowledgement of their impending disappearance. The images are of animals *receding* into a wildness that existed only in the imagination. There was, however, one 19th-century artist who was obsessed by the transformation about to take place, and whose work was an uncanny illustration of it. Grandville published his *Public and Private Life of Animals* in instalments between 1840 and 1842.

At first sight, Grandville's animals, dressed up and performing as men and women, appear to belong to the old tradition, whereby a person is portrayed as an animal so as to reveal more clearly an aspect of his or her character. The device was like putting on a mask, but its function was to unmask. The animal represents the apogee of the character trait in question: the lion, absolute courage: the hare, lechery. The animal once lived near the origin of the quality. It was through the animal that the quality first became recognizable. And so the animal lends it his name.

But as one goes on looking at Grandville's engravings, one becomes aware that the shock which they convey derives, in fact, from the opposite movement to that which one first assumed. These animals are not being 'borrowed' to explain people, nothing is being un-masked; on the contrary. These animals have become prisoners of a human/social situation into which they have been press-ganged. The vulture as landlord is more dreadfully rapacious than he is as a bird. The crocodiles at dinner are greedier at the table than they are in the river.

Here animals are not being used as reminders of origin, or as moral metaphors, they are being used *en masse* to 'people' situations. The movement that ends with the banality of Disney began as a disturbing, prophetic dream in the work of Grandville.

The dogs in Grandville's engraving of the dog-pound are in no way canine; they have dogs' faces, but what they are suffering is imprisonment *like men*.

The bear is a good father shows a bear dejectedly pulling a pram like any other human bread-winner. Grandville's first volume ends with the words 'Goodnight then, dear reader. Go home, lock your cage well, sleep tight and have pleasant dreams. Until tomorrow.' Animals and populace are becoming synonymous, which is to say the animals are fading away.

A later Grandville drawing, entitled *The animals enter-ing the steam ark*, is explicit. In the Judaeo-Christian tradition, Noah's Ark was the first ordered assembly of animals and man. The assembly is now over. Grandville shows us the great departure. On a quayside a long queue of different species is filing slowly away, their backs towards us. Their postures suggest all the last-minute doubts of emigrants. In the distance is a ramp by which the first have already entered the 19th-century ark, which is like an American steamboat. The bear. The lion. The donkey. The camel. The cock. The fox. Exeunt.

'About 1867,' according to the *London Zoo Guide*, 'a music hall artist called the Great Vance sang a song called *Walking in the zoo is the OK thing to do*, and the word "zoo" came into everyday use. London Zoo also brought the word "Jumbo" into the English language. Jumbo was an African elephant of mammoth size, who lived at the zoo between 1865 and 1882. Queen Victoria took an interest in him and eventually he ended his days as the star of the famous Barnum circus which travelled through America – his name living on to describe things of giant proportions.'

Public zoos came into existence at the beginning of the period which was to see the disappearance of animals from daily life. The zoo to which people go to meet animals, to observe them, to see them, is, in fact, a monument to the impossibility of such encounters. Modern zoos are an epitaph to a relationship which was as old as man. They are not seen as such because the wrong questions have been addressed to zoos.

When they were founded – the London Zoo in 1828, the Jardin des Plantes in 1793, the Berlin Zoo in 1844 – they brought considerable prestige to the national capitals. The prestige was not so different from that which had accrued to the private royal menageries. These menageries, along with gold plate, architecture, orchestras, players, furnishings, dwarfs, acrobats, uniforms, horses, art and food, had been demonstrations of an emperor's or king's power and wealth. Likewise in the 19th century, public zoos were an endorsement of modern colonial power. The capturing of the animals was a symbolic representation of the conquest of all distant and exotic lands. 'Explorers' proved their patriotism by sending home a tiger or an elephant. The gift of an exotic animal to the metropolitan zoo became a token in subservient diplomatic relations.

Yet, like every other 19th-century public institution, the zoo, however supportive of the ideology of imperialism, had to claim an independent and civic function. The claim was that it was another kind of museum, whose purpose was to further knowledge and public enlightenment. And so the first questions asked of zoos belonged to natural history; it was then thought possible to study the natural life of animals even in such unnatural conditions. A century later, more sophisticated zoologists such as Konrad Lorenz asked behaviouristic and ethological questions, the claimed purpose of which was to discover more about the springs of human action through the study of animals under experimental conditions.

Meanwhile, millions visited the zoos each year out of a curiosity which was both so large, so vague and so personal that it is hard to express in a single question. Today in France 22 million people visit the 200 zoos each year. A high proportion of the visitors were and are children.

Children in the industrialized world are surrounded

by animal imagery: toys, cartoons, pictures, decorations of every sort. No other source of imagery can begin to compete with that of animals. The apparently spontaneous interest that children have in animals might lead one to suppose that this has always been the case. Certainly some of the earliest toys (when toys were unknown to the vast majority of the population) were animal. Equally, children's games, all over the world, include real or pretended animals. Yet it was not until the 19th century that reproductions of animals became a regular part of the decor of middle-class childhoods – and then, in this century, with the advent of vast display and selling systems like Disney's – of all childhoods.

In the preceding centuries, the proportion of toys which were animal was small. And these did not pretend to realism, but were symbolic. The difference was that between a traditional hobby horse and a rocking horse: the first was merely a stick with a rudimentary head which children rode like a broom handle: the second was an elaborate 'reproduction' of a horse, painted realistically, with real reins of leather, a real mane of hair, and designed movement to resemble that of a horse galloping. The rocking horse was a 19th-century invention.

This new demand for verisimilitude in animal toys led to different methods of manufacture. The first stuffed animals were produced, and the most expensive were covered with real animal skin – usually the skin of still-born calves. The same period saw the appearance of soft animals – bears, tigers, rabbits – such as children take to bed with them. Thus the manufacture of realistic animal toys coincides, more or less, with the establishment of public zoos.

The family visit to the zoo is often a more sentimental occasion than a visit to a fair or a football match. Adults take children to the zoo to show them the originals of their 'reproductions', and also perhaps in the hope of re-finding some of the innocence of that reproduced animal world which they remember from their own childhood.

The animals seldom live up to the adults' memories, whilst to the children they appear, for the most part, unexpectedly lethargic and dull. (As frequent as the calls of animals in a zoo are the cries of children demanding: Where is he? Why doesn't he move? Is he dead?) And so one might summarize the felt, but not necessarily expressed, question of most visitors as: Why are these animals less than I believed?

And this unprofessional, unexpressed question is the one worth answering.

A zoo is a place where as many species and varieties of animal as possible are collected in order that they can be seen, observed, studied. In principle, each cage is a frame round the animal inside it. Visitors visit the zoo to look at animals. They proceed from cage to cage, not unlike visitors in an art gallery who stop in front of one painting, and then move on to the next or the one after next. Yet in the zoo the view is always wrong. Like an image out of focus. One is so accustomed to this that one scarcely notices it any more; or, rather, the apology habitually anticipates the disappointment, so that the latter is not felt. And the apology runs like this: What do you expect? It's not a dead object you have come to look at, it's alive. It's leading its own life. Why should this coincide with its being properly visible? Yet the reasoning of this apology is inadequate. The truth is more startling.

However you look at these animals, even if the animal is up against the bars, less than a foot from you, looking outwards in the public direction, *you are looking at something that has been rendered absolutely marginal*; and all the concentration you can muster will never be enough to centralize it. Why is this?

Within limits, the animals are free, but both they themselves, and their spectators, presume on their close confinement. The visibility through the glass, the spaces between the bars, or the empty air above the moat, are not what they seem – if they were, then everything would be changed. Thus visibility, space, air, have been reduced to tokens.

The decor, accepting these elements as tokens, sometimes reproduces them to create pure illusion – as in the case of painted prairies or painted rock pools at the back of the boxes for small animals. Sometimes it merely adds further tokens to suggest something of the animal's original landscape – the dead branches of a tree for monkeys, artificial rocks for bears, pebbles and shallow water for crocodiles. These added tokens serve two distinct purposes: for the spectator they are like theatre props: for the animal they constitute the bare minimum of an environment in which they can physically exist.

The animals, isolated from each other and without interaction between species, have become utterly dependent upon their keepers. Consequently most of their responses have been changed. What was central to their interest has been replaced by a passive waiting for a series of arbitrary outside interventions. The events they perceive occurring around them have become as illusory in terms of their natural responses as the painted prairies. At the same time this very isolation (usually) guarantees their longevity as specimens and facilitates their taxonomic arrangement.

All this is what makes them marginal. The space which they inhabit is artificial. Hence their tendency to bundle towards the edge of it. (Beyond its edges there may be real space.) In some cages the light is equally artificial. In all cases the environment is illusory. Nothing surrounds them except their own lethargy or hyperactivity. They have nothing to act upon – except, briefly, supplied food and – very occasionally – a supplied mate. (Hence their perennial actions become marginal actions without an object.) Lastly, their dependence and isolation have so conditioned their responses that they treat any event which takes place around them – usually it is in front of them, where the public is – as marginal. (Hence their assumption of an otherwise exclusively human attitude – indifference.)

Zoos, realistic animal toys and the widespread commercial diffusion of animal imagery, all began as animals started to be withdrawn from daily life. One could suppose that such innovations were compensatory. Yet in reality the innovations themselves belonged to the same remorseless movement as was dispersing the animals. The zoos, with their theatrical decor for display, were in fact demonstrations of how animals had been rendered absolutely marginal. The realistic toys increased the demand for the new animal puppet: the urban pet. The reproduction of animals in images – as their biological reproduction in birth becomes a rarer and rarer sight – was competitively forced to make animals ever more exotic and remote.

Everywhere animals disappear. In zoos they constitute the living monument to their own disappearance. And in doing so, they provoked their last metaphor. *The Naked Ape, The Human Zoo*, are titles of world bestsellers. In these books the zoologist, Desmond Morris, proposes that the unnatural behaviour of animals in captivity can help us to understand, accept and overcome the stresses involved in living in consumer societies.

All sites of enforced marginalization – ghettos, shanty towns, prisons, madhouses, concentration camps – have something in common with zoos. But it is both too easy and too evasive to use the zoo as a symbol. The zoo is a demonstration of the relations between man and animals; nothing else. The marginalization of animals is today being followed by the marginalization and disposal of the only class who, throughout history, has remained familiar with animals and maintained the wisdom which accompanies that familiarity: the middle and small peasant. The basis of this wisdom is an acceptance of the dualism at the very origin of the relation between man and animal. The rejection of this dualism is probably an important factor in opening the way to modern totalitarianism. But I do not wish to go beyond the limits of that unprofessional, unexpressed but fundamental question asked of the zoo.

The zoo cannot but disappoint. The public purpose of zoos is to offer visitors the opportunity of looking at animals. Yet nowhere in a zoo can a stranger encounter the look of an animal. At the most, the animal's gaze flickers and passes on. They look sideways. They look blindly beyond. They scan mechanically. They have been immunized to encounter, because nothing can any more occupy a *central* place in their attention.

Therein lies the ultimate consequence of their marginalization. That look between animal and man, which may have played a crucial role in the development of human society, and with which, in any case, all men had always lived until less than a century ago, has been extinguished. Looking at each animal, the unaccompanied zoo visitor is alone. As for the crowds, they belong to a species which has at last been isolated.

This historic loss, to which zoos are a monument, is now irredeemable for the culture of capitalism.

1977

Ape Theatre

In memory of Peter Fuller and our many conversations about the chain of being and Neo-Darwinism

In Basel the zoo is almost next to the railway station. Most of the larger birds in the zoo are free-flying, and so it can happen that you see a stork or a cormorant flying home over the marshalling yards. Equally unexpected is the ape house. It is constructed like a circular theatre with three stages: one for the gorillas, another for the orang-utans and a third for the chimpanzees.

You take your place on one of the tiers – as in a Greek theatre – or you can go to the very front of the pit, and press your forehead against the soundproof plate glass. The lack of sound makes the spectacle on the other side, in a certain way, sharper, like mime. It also allows the apes to be less bothered by the public. We are mute to them too.

All my life I've visited zoos, perhaps because going to the zoo is one of my few happy childhood memories. My father used to take me. We didn't talk much, but we shared each other's pleasure, and I was well aware that his was largely based on mine. We used to watch the apes together, losing all sense of time, each of us, in his fashion, pondering the mystery of progeniture. My mother, on the rare occasions she came with us, refused the higher primates. She preferred the newly found pandas.

I tried to persuade her, but she would reply, following her own logic: 'I'm a vegetarian and I only gave it up, the practice not the principle, for the sake of you boys and for Daddy.' Bears were another animal she liked. Apes, I can see now, reminded her of the passions which lead to the spilling of blood.

The audience in Basel is of all ages. From toddlers to pensioners. No other spectacle in the world can attract such a wide spectrum of the public. Some sit, like my father and I once did, lost to the passing of time. Others drop in for a few moments. There are habitués who come every day and whom the actors recognize. But on nobody – not even the youngest toddler – is the dramatic evolutionary riddle lost: how is it that they are so like us and yet not us?

This is the question which dominates the dramas on each of the three stages. Today the gorillas' play is a social one about coming to terms with imprisonment. Life sentences. The chimpanzees' is cabaret, for each performer has her or his own number. The orang-utans' is *Werther* without words – soulful and dreamy. I am exaggerating? Of course, because I do not yet know how to define the real drama of the theatre in Basel.

Is theatre possible without an awareness of re-enactment, which is related to a sense of death? Probably not. But perhaps both, almost, exist here.

Each stage has at least one private recess where an animal can go if she or he wishes to leave the public. From time to time they do so. Sometimes for quite long periods. When they come out to face the audience again, they are perhaps not so far from a practice of re-enactment. In the London zoo chimps pretended to eat and drink off invisible plates with nonexistent glasses. A pantomime.

As for a sense of death, chimpanzees are as familiar as we are with fear, and the Dutch zoologist Dr Kortlaudt believes they have intimations of mortality.

In the first half of the century there were attempts to teach chimpanzees to talk – until it was discovered that the form of their vocal tract was unsuitable for the production of the necessary range of sounds. Later they were taught a deaf and dumb language, and a chimp called Washoe in Ellensburg, Washington, called a duck a water bird. Did this mean that Washoe had broken through a language barrier, or had she just learnt by rote? A heated debate followed (the distinction of man was at stake!) about what does or does not constitute a language for animals.

It was already known – thanks to the extraordinary work of Jane Goodall, who lived with her chimpanzees in the wild in Tanzania – that these animals used tools, and that, language or no language, their ability to communicate with one another was both wide-ranging and subtle.

Another chimpanzee in the United States named Sarah underwent a series of tests, conducted by Douglas Gillan, which were designed to show whether or not she could reason. Contrary to what Descartes believed, a verbal language may not be indispensable for the process of reasoning. Sarah was shown a video of her trainer playing the part of being locked in a cage and desperately trying to get out! After the film she was offered a series of pictures of varying objects to choose from. One, for instance, showed a lighted match. The picture she chose was of a key – the only object which would have been useful for the situation she had seen enacted on the video screen.

In Basel we are watching a strange theatre in which, on both sides of the glass, the performers may believe they are an audience. On both sides the drama begins with resemblance and the uneasy relationship that exists between resemblance and closeness.

The idea of evolution is very old. Hunters believed that animals – and especially the ones they hunted – were in some mysterious way their brothers. Aristotle argued that all the forms of nature constituted a series, a chain of being, which began with the simple and became more and more complex, striving towards the perfect. In Latin *evolution* means unfolding.

A group of handicapped patients from a local institution come into the theatre. Some have to be helped up the tiers, others manage by themselves, one or two are in wheelchairs. They form a different kind of audience – or rather, an audience with different reactions. They are less puzzled, less astounded, but more amused. Like children? Not at all. They are less puzzled because they are more familiar with what is out of the ordinary. Or, to put it another way, their sense of the norm is far wider.

What was new and outrageous in *The Origin of Species* when it was first published in 1859 was Darwin's argument that all animal species had evolved from the same prototype, and that this immensely slow evolution had taken place through certain accidental mutations being favoured by natural selection, which had worked according to the principle of the survival of the fittest. A series of accidents. Without design or purpose and without experience counting. (Darwin rejected Lamarck's thesis that acquired characteristics could be inherited.) The pre-condition for Darwin's theory being plausible was something even more shocking: the wastes of empty time required: about 500 million years!

Until the nineteenth century it was generally, if not universally, believed that the world was a few thousand years old – something that could be measured by the time scale of human generations. (As in Genesis, chapter 5.) But in 1830 Charles Lyell published *The Principles of Geology* and proposed that the earth, with 'no vestige of a beginning – no prospect of an end', was millions, perhaps hundreds of millions of years old.

Darwin's thinking was a creative response to the terrifying immensity of what had just been opened up. And the sadness of Darwinism – for no other scientific revolution, when it was made, broadcast so little hope – derived, I think, from the desolation of the distances involved.

The sadness, the desolation, is there in the last sentence of *The Descent of Man*, published in 1871: 'We must, however, acknowledge, as it seems to me, that man with all his noble qualities, still bears in his bodily frame the indelible stamp of his lowly origin.'

'The indelible stamp' speaks volumes. 'Indelible' in the sense that (unfortunately) it cannot be washed out. 'Stamp' meaning 'brand, mark, stain'. And in the word 'lowly' during the nineteenth century, as in Thatcher's Britain, there is shame.

The liberty of the newly opened-up space-time of the universe brought with it a feeling of insignificance and *pudeur*, from which the best that could be redeemed was the virtue of intellectual courage, the virtue of being unflinching. And courageous the thinkers of that time were!

Whenever an actor who is not a baby wants to piss or shit, he or she gets up and goes to the edge of a balcony or deck, and there defecates or urinates below, so as to remain clean. An habitual act which we seldom see enacted on the stage. And the effect is surprising. The public watch with a kind of pride. An altogether legitimate one. Don't shit yourself. Soon we'll be entering another century.

Mostly, the thinkers of the nineteenth century thought mechanically, for theirs was the century of machines. They thought in terms of chains, branches, lines, comparative anatomies, clockworks, grids. They knew about power, resistance, speed, competition. Consequently, they discovered a great deal about the material world, about tools and production. What they knew less about is what we still don't know much about: the way brains work. I can't get this out of my mind: it's somewhere at the centre of the theatre we're watching.

Apes don't live entirely within the needs and impulses of their own bodies – like the cats do. (It may be different in the wild, but this is true on the stage.) They have a gratuitous curiosity. All animals play, but the others play at being themselves, whereas the apes experiment. They suffer from a surplus of curiosity. They can momentarily forget their needs, or any single unchanging role. A young female will pretend to be a mother cuddling a baby lent by its real mother. 'Baby-sitting,' the zoologists call it.

Their surplus of curiosity, their research (every animal searches, only apes research) make them suffer in two evident ways – and probably also in others, invisibly. Their bodies, forgotten, suddenly nag, twinge, and irritate. They become impatient with their own skin – like Marat suffering from eczema.

And then too, starved of events, they suffer boredom. Baudelaire's *l'ennui*. Not at the same level of self-doubt, but nevertheless with pain, apathy. The signs of boredom may resemble those of simple drowsiness. But *l'ennui* has its unmistakable lassitude. The body, instead of relaxing, huddles, the eyes stare painfully without focus, the hands, finding nothing new to touch or do, become like gloves worn by a creature drowning.

'If it could be demonstrated,' Darwin wrote, 'that any complex organ existed which could not possibly have been formed by numerous, successive slight modifications, my theory would absolutely break down.'

If the apes are partly victims of their own bodies – the

price they pay, like man, for not being confined to their immediate needs – they have found a consolation, which Europe has forgotten. My mother used to say the chimps were looking for fleas, and that when they found one, they put it between their teeth and bit it. But it goes further than Mother thought – as I guessed even then. The chimpanzees touch and caress and scratch each other for hours on end (and according to the etiquette rules of a strict group hierarchy) not only hygienically, to catch parasites, but to give pleasure. 'Grooming', as it is called, is one of their principal ways of appeasing the troublesome body.

This one is scratching inside her ear with her little finger. Now she has stopped scratching to examine minutely her small nail. Her gestures are intimately familiar and strikingly remote. (The same is true for most actions on any theatre stage.) An orang-utan is preparing a bed for herself. Suddenly, she hesitates before placing her armful of straw on the floor, as if she has heard a siren. Not only are the apes' functional gestures familiar, but also their expressive ones. Gestures which denote surprise, amusement, tenderness, irritation, pleasure, indifference, desire, fear.

But they move differently. A male gorilla is sitting at ease with his arm held straight and high above his head; and for him this position is as relaxed as sitting with legs crossed is for women and men. Everything which derives from the apes' skill in swinging from branches – *brachiation*, as the zoologists call it – sets them apart. Tarzan only swung from vines – he never used his hanging arms like legs, walking sideways.

In evolutionary history, however, this difference is in fact a link. Monkeys walk on all fours along the tops of branches and use their tails for hanging. The common ancestors of man and apes began, instead, to use their arms – began to become *brachiators*. This, the theory goes, gave them the advantage of being able to reach fruit at the ends of branches!

I must have been two years old when I had my first cuddly toy. It was a monkey. A chimpanzee, in fact. I think I called him Jackie. To be certain, I'd have to ask my mother. She would remember. But my mother is dead. There is just a chance – one in a hundred million (about the same as a chance mutation being favoured by natural selection) – that a reader may be able to tell me, for we had visitors to our home in Higham's Park, in East London, sixty years ago, and I presented my chimp to everyone who came through the front door. I think his name was Jackie.

Slowly, the hanging position, favoured by natural selection, changed the anatomy of the brachiators' torsos so that finally they became half-upright animals – although not yet as upright as humans. It is thanks to hanging from trees that we have long collarbones which keep our arms away from our chests, wrists which allow our hands to bend backwards and sideways, and shoulder sockets that let our arms rotate.

It is thanks to hanging from trees that one of the actors can throw himself into the arms of a mother and cry. Brachiation gave us breasts to beat and to be held against. No other animal can do these things.

*

When Darwin thought about the eyes of mammals, he admitted that he broke out in a cold sweat. The complexity of the eye was hard to explain within the logic of his theory, for it implied the co-ordination of so many evolutionary 'accidents'. If the eye is to work at all, all the elements have to be there: tear glands, eyelid, cornea, pupil, retina, millions of light-sensitive rods and cones which transmit to the brain millions of electrical impulses per second. Before they constituted an eye, these intricate parts would have been useless, so why should they have been favoured by natural selection? The existence of the eye perfidiously suggests an evolutionary aim, an intention.

Darwin finally got over the problem by going back to the existence of light-sensitive spots on one-celled organisms. These, he claimed, could have been 'the first eye' from which the evolution of our complex eyes first began.

I have the impression that the oldest gorilla may be blind. Like Beckett's Pozzo. I ask his keeper, a young woman with fair hair. Yes, she says, he's almost blind. How old is he? I ask. She looks at me hard. About your age, she replies, in his early sixties.

Recently, molecular biologists have shown that we share with apes 99 per cent of their DNA. Only 1 per cent of his genetic code separates man from the chimpanzee or the gorilla. The orang-utan, which means in the language of the people of Borneo 'man of the forest', is fractionally further removed. If we take another animal family, in order to emphasize how small the 1 per cent is, a dog differs from a raccoon by 12 per cent. The genetic closeness between man and ape – apart from making our theatre possible – strongly suggests that their common ancestor existed not 20 million years ago as the Neo-Darwinist palaeontologists believed, but maybe only 4 million years ago. This molecular evidence has been contested because there are no fossil proofs to support it. But in evolutionary theory fossils, it seems to me, have usually been notable by their absence!

In the Anglo-Saxon world today the Creationists, who take the Genesis story of the Creation as the literal truth, are increasingly vocal and insist that their version be taught in schools alongside the Neo-Darwinist one. The orang-utan is like he is, say the Creationists, because that's the way God made him, once and for all, five thousand years ago! He is like he is, reply the Neo-Darwinists, because he has been efficient in the ceaseless struggle for survival!

Her orang-utan eyes operate exactly like mine – each retina with its 130 million rods and cones. But her expression is the oldest I've ever seen. Approach it at your peril, for you can fall into a kind of maelstrom of ageing. The plunge is still there in Jean Mohr's photo.

Not far up the Rhine from Basel, Angelus Silesius, the seventeenth-century German doctor of medicine, studied in Strasbourg, and he once wrote:

Anybody who passes more than a day in eternity is as old as God could ever be.

I look at her with her eyelids which are so pale that when she closes them they're like eyecups, and I wonder.

Certain Neo-Darwinist ideas are intriguing: Bolk's theory of neoteny, for instance. According to Bolk, 'man in his bodily development is a primate foetus that has become sexually mature', and consequently can reproduce. His theory proposes that a genetic code can stop one kind of growth and encourage another. Man is a neonate ape to whom this happened. Unfinished, he is able to learn more.

It has even been argued that today's apes may be descendants of a hominid, and that in them the neoteny brake was taken off so that they stopped stopping at the foetus stage, grew body hair again and were born with tough skulls! This would make them more modern than we are.

Yet in general, the conceptual framework in which the Neo-Darwinists and the Creationists debate is of such limited imagination that the contrast with the immensity of the process whose origin they are searching is flagrant. They are like two bands of seven-year-olds who, having discovered a packet of love letters in an attic, try to piece together the story behind the correspondence. Both bands are ingenious and argue ferociously with one another, but the passion of the letters is beyond their competence.

Perhaps it is objectively true that only poetry can talk of birth and origin. Because true poetry invokes the whole of language (it breathes with everything it has not said), just as the origin invokes the whole of life, the whole of Being.

The mother orang-utan has come back, this time with her baby. She is sitting right up against the glass. The children in the audience have come close to watch her. Suddenly, I think of a Madonna and Child by Cosimo Tura. I'm not indulging in a sentimental confusion. I haven't forgotten I'm talking about apes any more than I've forgotten I'm watching a theatre. The more one emphasizes the millions of years, the more extraordinary the expressive gestures become. Arms, fingers, eyes, always eyes . . . A certain way of being protective, a certain gentleness – if one could feel the fingers on one's neck, one would say a certain *tenderness* – which has endured for five million years.

A species that did not protect its young would not survive, comes the answer. Indisputably. But the answer does not explain the theatre.

I ask myself about the theatre – about its mystery and its essence. It's to do with time. The theatre, more tangibly than any other art, presents us with the past. Paintings may show what the past looked like, but they are like traces or footprints, they no longer move. With each theatre performance, what once happened is re-enacted. Each time we keep the same rendezvous: with Macbeth who can't wake up from his downfall; with Antigone who must do her duty. And each night in the theatre Antigone, who died three millennia ago, says: 'We have only a short time to please the living, all eternity to please the dead.'

Theatre depends upon two times physically co-existing. The hour of the performance and the moment of the drama. If you read a novel, you leave the present; in the theatre you never leave the present. The past becomes the present in the only way that it is possible for this to happen. And this unique possibility is theatre.

The Creationists, like all bigots, derive their fervour from rejection – the more they can reject, the more righteous they themselves feel. The Neo-Darwinists are trapped within the machine of their theory, in which there can be no place for creation as an act of love. (Their theory was born of the nineteenth century, the most orphaned of centuries.)

The ape theatre in Basel, with its two times, suggests an alternative view. The evolutionary process unfolded, more or less as the evolutionists suppose, within time. The fabric of its duration has been stretched to breaking point by billions of years. Outside time, God is still (present tense) creating the universe.

Silesius, after he left Strasbourg to return to Cracow, wrote: 'God is still creating the world. Does that seem strange to you? You must suppose that in him there is no before nor after, as there is here.'

How can the timeless enter the temporal? the gorilla now asks me.

Can we think of time as a field magnetized by eternity? I'm no scientist. (As I say that, I can see the real ones smiling!)

Which are they?

The ones up there on a ladder, looking for something. Now they're coming down to take a bow . . .

As I say, I'm no scientist, but I have the impression that scientists today, when dealing with phenomena whose time or spatial scale is either immense or very small (a full set of human genes contains about 6 billion bases: bases being the units – the signs – of the genetic language), are on the point of breaking through space-time to discover another axis on which events may be strung, and that, in face of the hidden scales of nature, they resort increasingly to the model of a brain or mind to explain the universe.

'Can't God find what he is looking for?' To this question Silesius replied, 'From eternity he is searching for what is lost, far from him, in time.'

The orang-utan mother presses the baby's head against her chest.

Birth begins the process of learning to be separate. The separation is hard to believe or accept. Yet, as we accept it, our imagination grows – imagination which is the capacity to reconnect, to bring together, that which is separate. Metaphor finds the traces which indicate that all is one. Acts of solidarity, compassion, self-sacrifice, generosity are attempts to re-establish – or at least a refusal to forget – a once-known unity. Death is the hardest test of accepting the separation which life has incurred.

You're playing with words!

Who said that?

Jackie!

The act of creation implies a separation. Something that remains attached to the creator is only half-created. To create is to let take over something which did not exist before, and is therefore new. And the new is inseparable from pain, for it is alone.

One of the male chimps is suddenly angry. Histrionically. Everything he can pick up he throws. He tries to pull down the stage trees. He is like Samson at the temple. But unlike Samson, he is not high up in the group hierarchy of the cage. The other actors are nonetheless impressed by his fury.

Alone, we are forced to recognize that we have been created, like everything else. Only our souls, when encouraged, remember the origin, wordlessly.

Silesius's master was Eckardt, who, further down the Rhine beyond Strasbourg, in Cologne, wrote during the thirteenth century, 'God becomes God when the animals say: God.'

Are these the words which the play behind the sound-proof plate glass is about?

In any case I can't find better.

1990

The White Bird

From time to time I have been invited by institutions – mostly American – to speak about aesthetics. On one occasion I considered accepting and I thought of taking with me a bird made of white wood. But I didn't go. The problem is that you can't talk about aesthetics without talking about the principle of hope and the existence of evil. During the long winters the peasants in certain parts of the Haute Savoie used to make wooden birds to hang in their kitchens and perhaps also in their chapels. Friends who are travellers have told me that they have seen similar birds, made according to the same principle, in certain regions of Czechoslovakia, Russia and the Baltic countries. The tradition may be more widespread.

The principle of the construction of these birds is simple enough, although to make a fine bird demands considerable skill. You take two bars of pine wood, about six inches in length, a little less than one inch in height and the same in width. You soak them in water so that the wood has the maximum pliability, then you carve them. One piece will be the head and body with a fan tail, the second piece will represent the wings. The art principally concerns the making of the wing and tail feathers. The whole block of each wing is carved according to the silhouette of a single feather. Then the block is sliced into thirteen thin layers and these are gently opened out, one by one, to make a fan shape. Likewise for the second wing and for the tail feathers. The two pieces of wood are joined together to form a cross and the bird is complete. No glue is used and there is only one nail where the two pieces of wood cross. Very light, weighing only two or three ounces, the birds are usually hung on a thread from an overhanging mantelpiece or beam so that they move with the air currents.

It would be absurd to compare one of these birds to a Van Gogh self-portrait or a Rembrandt crucifixion. They are simple, home-made objects, worked according to a traditional pattern. Yet, by their very simplicity, they allow one to categorize the qualities which make them pleasing and mysterious to everyone who sees them.

First there is a figurative representation – one is looking at a bird, more precisely a dove, apparently hanging in mid-air. Thus, there is a reference to the surrounding world of nature. Secondly, the choice of subject (a flying bird) and the context in which it is placed (indoors where live birds are unlikely) render the object symbolic. This primary symbolism then joins a more general, cultural one. Birds, and doves in particular, have been credited with symbolic meanings in a very wide variety of cultures.

Thirdly, there is a respect for the material used. The wood has been fashioned according to its own qualities of lightness, pliability and texture. Looking at it, one is surprised by how well wood becomes bird. Fourthly, there is a formal unity and economy. Despite the object's apparent complexity, the grammar of its making is

simple, even austere. Its richness is the result of rep-
etitions which are also variations. Fifthly, this man-made
object provokes a kind of astonishment: how on earth
was it made? I have given rough indications above, but
anyone unfamiliar with the technique wants to take the
dove in his hands and examine it closely to discover the
secret which lies behind its making.

These five qualities, when undifferentiated and perceived as a whole, provoke at least a momentary sense
of being before a mystery. One is looking at a piece of
wood that has become a bird. One is looking at a bird
that is somehow more than a bird. One is looking at
something that has been worked with a mysterious skill
and a kind of love.

Thus far I have tried to isolate the qualities of the
white bird which provoke an aesthetic emotion. (The
word 'emotion', although designating a motion of the
heart and of the imagination, is somewhat confusing for
we are considering an emotion that has little to do with
the others we experience, notably because the self here
is in a far greater degree of abeyance.) Yet my definitions
beg the essential question. They reduce aesthetics to art.
They say nothing about the relation between art and
nature, art and the world.

Before a mountain, a desert just after the sun has gone
down, or a fruit tree, one can also experience aesthetic
emotion. Consequently we are forced to begin again –
not this time with a man-made object but with the nature
into which we are born.

Urban living has always tended to produce a sentimental view of nature. Nature is thought of as a garden, or

a view framed by a window, or as an arena of freedom. Peasants, sailors, nomads have known better. Nature is energy and struggle. It is what exists without any promise. If it can be thought of by man as an arena, a setting, it has to be thought of as one which lends itself as much to evil as to good. Its energy is fearsomely indifferent. The first necessity of life is shelter. Shelter against nature. The first prayer is for protection. The first sign of life is pain. If the Creation was purposeful, its purpose is a hidden one which can only be discovered intangibly within signs, never by the evidence of what happens.

It is within this bleak natural context that beauty is encountered, and the encounter is by its nature sudden and unpredictable. The gale blows itself out, the sea changes from the colour of grey shit to aquamarine. Under the fallen boulder of an avalanche a flower grows. Over the shanty town the moon rises. I offer dramatic examples so as to insist upon the bleakness of the context. Reflect upon more everyday examples. However it is encountered, beauty is always an exception, always *in despite of*. This is why it moves us.

It can be argued that the origin of the way we are moved by natural beauty was functional. Flowers are a promise of fertility, a sunset is a reminder of fire and warmth, moonlight makes the night less dark, the bright colours of a bird's plumage are (atavistically even for us) a sexual stimulus. Yet such an argument is too reductionist, I believe. Snow is useless. A butterfly offers us very little.

Of course the range of what a given community

finds beautiful in nature will depend upon its means of survival, its economy, its geography. What Eskimos find beautiful is unlikely to be the same as what the Ashanti found beautiful. Within modern class societies there are complex ideological determinations: we know, for instance, that the British ruling class in the eighteenth century disliked the sight of the sea. Equally, the social use to which an aesthetic emotion may be put changes according to the historical moment: the silhouette of a mountain can represent the home of the dead or a challenge to the initiative of the living. Anthropology, comparative studies of religion, political economy and Marxism have made all this clear.

Yet there seem to be certain constants which all cultures have found 'beautiful': among them – certain flowers, trees, forms of rock, birds, animals, the moon, running water . . .

One is obliged to acknowledge a coincidence or perhaps a congruence. The evolution of natural forms and the evolution of human perception have coincided to produce the phenomenon of a potential recognition: what *is* and what we can see (and by seeing also feel) sometimes meet at a point of affirmation. This point, this coincidence, is two-faced: what has been seen is recognized and affirmed and, at the same time, the seer is affirmed by what he sees. For a brief moment one finds oneself – without the pretensions of a creator – in the position of God in the first chapter of Genesis . . . And he saw that *it was* good. The aesthetic emotion before nature derives, I believe, from this double affirmation.

Yet we do not live in the first chapter of Genesis. We live – if one follows the biblical sequence of events – after the Fall. In any case, we live in a world of suffering in which evil is rampant, a world whose events do not confirm our Being, a world that has to be resisted. It is in this situation that the aesthetic moment offers hope. That we find a crystal or a poppy beautiful means that we are less alone, that we are more deeply inserted into existence than the course of a single life would lead us to believe. I try to describe as accurately as possible the experience in question; my starting point is phenomeno-logical, not deductive; its form, perceived as such, becomes a message that one receives but cannot translate because, in it, all is instantaneous. For an instant, the energy of one's perception becomes inseparable from the energy of the creation.

The aesthetic emotion we feel before a man-made object – such as the white bird with which I started – is a derivative of the emotion we feel before nature. The white bird is an attempt to translate a message received from a real bird. All the languages of art have been developed as an attempt to transform the instantaneous into the permanent. Art supposes that beauty is not an exception – is not *in despite of* – but is the basis for an order.

Several years ago, when considering the historical face of art, I wrote that I judged a work according to whether or not it helped men in the modern world claim their social rights. I hold to that. Art's other, transcendental face raises the question of man's ontological right.

The notion that art is the mirror of nature is one that

only appeals in periods of scepticism. Art does not imitate nature, it imitates a creation, sometimes to propose an alternative world, sometimes simply to amplify, to confirm, to make social the brief hope offered by nature. Art is an organized response to what nature allows us to glimpse occasionally. Art sets out to transform the potential recognition into an unceasing one. It proclaims man in the hope of receiving a surer reply ... the transcendental face of art is always a form of prayer.

The white wooden bird is wafted by the warm air rising from the stove in the kitchen where the neighbours are drinking. Outside, in minus 25°C, the real birds are freezing to death!

1985

The Eaters and the Eaten

'The consumer society', so often and widely discussed as if it were a relatively new phenomenon, is the logical outcome of economic and technological processes which began at least a hundred years ago. Consumerism is intrinsic to nineteenth-century bourgeois culture. Consumption fulfils a cultural as well as an economic need. The nature of this need becomes clearer if we look at the most direct and simple form of consumption: eating.

How does the bourgeois approach his food? If we isolate and define this specific approach we will be able to recognize it when it is far more widely diffused.

The question could become complex because of national and historical differences. The French bourgeois attitude to food is not the same as the English. A German mayor sits down to his dinner with a somewhat different attitude from a Greek mayor. A fashionable banquet in Rome is not quite the same as one in Copenhagen. Many of the eating habits and attitudes described in Trollope and Balzac are no longer to be found anywhere.

Nevertheless an overall view, an outline, emerges if one compares the bourgeois manner of eating with the one, within the same geographical areas, from which it is most distinct: the peasant manner of eating. Working-class eating habits have less tradition than those of the other two classes because they are far more vulnerable to fluctuations of the economy.

On a world scale, the distinction between bourgeois and peasant is closely related to the brute contrast between plenty and scarcity. This contrast amounts to a war. But, for our limited purpose now, the distinction is not between the hungry and the overfed, but between two traditional views of the value of food, the significance of the meal and the act of eating.

At the outset it is worth noting a conflict in the bourgeois view. On the one hand, meals have a regular and symbolic importance in the life of the bourgeois. On the other hand, he considers that to discuss eating is frivolous. This article, for example, cannot by its nature be serious; and if it takes itself seriously, it is pretentious. Cookbooks are bestsellers and most newspapers have their food columns. But what they discuss is considered a mere embellishment and is (mostly) the domain of women. The bourgeois does not think of the act of eating as a fundamental one.

The principal regular meal. For the peasant this meal is usually at midday; for the bourgeois it is usually dinner in the evening. The practical reasons for this are so obvious that they need not be listed. What may be significant is that the peasant meal is in the middle of the day, surrounded by work. It is placed in the day's stomach. The bourgeois meal comes after the day's work and marks the transition between day and evening. It is closer to the day's head (if the day begins with getting to the feet) and to dreams.

At the peasant's table the relationship between implements, food and eaters is intimate, and a value is conferred on use and handling. Each person has his own knife which he may well take out of his pocket. The knife is worn, used for many purposes other than eating, and usefully sharp. Whenever possible the same plate is kept throughout the meal, and between dishes it is cleaned with bread which is eaten. Each eater takes his share of the food and drink which are placed before all. For example: he holds the bread to his body, cuts a piece of it towards himself, and puts the bread down for another. Likewise with cheese or sausage. Contiguity as between uses, users and foods is treated as natural. There is a minimum of division.

On the bourgeois table everything that can be is kept untouched and separate. Every dish has its own cutlery and plate. In general plates are not cleaned by eating – because eating and cleaning are distinct activities. Each eater (or a servant) holds the serving dish to allow another to serve himself. The meal is a series of discrete, untouched gifts.

To the peasant all food represents work accomplished. The work may or may not have been his own or that of his family, but if it isn't, the work represented is nevertheless directly exchangeable with his own work. Because food represents physical work, the eater's body already 'knows' the food it is going to eat. (The peasant's strong resistance to eating any 'foreign' food for the first time is partly because its origin in the work process is unknown.) He does not expect to be surprised by food – except, sometimes, by its quality. His food is familiar like his own body. Its action on his body is *continuous* with the previous action of the body (labour) on the food. He eats in the room in which the food is prepared and cooked.

To the bourgeois, food is not directly exchangeable with his own work or activities. (The quality attributable to home-grown vegetables becomes exceptional.) Food is a commodity he buys. Meals, even when cooked at home, are purchased through a cash exchange. The purchase is delivered in a special room: the domestic dining-room, or restaurant. This room has no other purpose. It always has at least two doors or ways of entry. One door connects with his own daily life; through it he has entered in order to be served with food. The second door connects with the kitchen; through it the food is brought out and the waste is taken away. Thus, in the dining-room, food is abstracted from its own production and from the 'real' world of his daily activities. Behind the two doors lie secrets: secrets of recipes behind the kitchen door; professional or personal secrets, not to be discussed at table, behind the other.

Abstracted, framed, insulated, the eaters and what is eaten form an isolated moment. This moment has to create its own content out of the air. The content tends to be theatrical: the décor of the table with its silver, glass, linen, china, etc.; the lighting; the relative formality of dress; the careful seating arrangements whenever there are guests; the ritualistic etiquette of table manners; the formality of serving; the transformation of the table between each act (course); and, finally, the leaving of the theatre together for a more dispersed and informal setting.

The Eaters and the Eaten

To the peasant, food represents work done and therefore repose. The fruit of labour is not only the 'fruit' but also the time taken from work time, spent in eating the food. Feasts apart, he accepts at table the sedative effect of eating. The appetite, satisfied, is quietened.

To the bourgeois the drama of eating, far from being reposeful, is a stimulus. The theatrical invitation of the scene often provokes family dramas at meal times. The scene of the typical oedipal drama is not, as logically it might be, the bedroom, but the dinner table. The dining-room is the place of assembly where the bourgeois family appears to itself in public guise, and where its conflicting interests and power struggles are pursued in a highly formalized manner. The ideal bourgeois drama, however, is entertainment. The use of the word 'entertain' meaning to invite guests is significant here. Yet entertainment always proposes its opposite: boredom. Boredom haunts the insulated dining-room. Hence the conscious emphasis placed on dinner talk, wit and conversation. But the spectre of boredom also characterizes the way of eating.

The bourgeois overeats. Especially meat. A psychosomatic explanation may be that his highly developed sense of competition compels him to protect himself with a source of energy – proteins. (Just as his children protect themselves from the emotional cold with sweets.) The cultural explanation, however, is as important. If the scale of the meal is *spectacular*, all the eaters share in its achievement, and boredom is less likely. The shared achievement is not, fundamentally, culinary. The achievement is that of wealth. What wealth has obtained from nature is an affidavit that overproduction and infinite increase are natural. The variety, the quantity, the waste of food prove the *naturalness* of wealth.

In the nineteenth century with partridge, mutton and porridge for breakfast (in England), and three meats and two fish for dinner, the quantities were net, the proof extracted from nature arithmetical. Today with modern means of transport and refrigeration, the accelerated pace of daily life and a different use of the 'servant' classes, the spectacular is achieved in another way. The most varied and exotic foods are acquired out of season, and the dishes come from all over the world. Canard à la Chinoise is placed beside Steak Tartare and Boeuf Bourguignon. The affidavit obtained is no longer just from nature concerning quantity. It is also from history to testify how wealth unites the world.

By using the vomitorium the Romans separated the palate from the stomach in the pursuit of 'pleasure'. The bourgeois separates the act of eating from the body so that it can become, first, a spectacular social claim. The significance of the act of eating asparagus is not: I am eating this with pleasure; but: we *can* eat this here and now. The typical bourgeois meal is for each eater a series of discrete gifts. Each gift should be a surprise. But the message in each gift is the same: *happy the world which feeds you*.

The distinction between the principal regular meal and the celebration or feast is very clear for the peasant, and often blurred for the bourgeois. (Which is why some of what I have written above borders, for the bourgeois, on the feast.) For the peasant what he eats and how he eats daily are continuous with the rest of his life. The rhythm of this life is cyclic. The repetition of meals is similar to, and connected with, the repetition of the seasons. His diet is local and seasonal. And so the foods available, the methods of cooking them, the variations in his diet, mark recurring moments throughout a lifetime. To become bored with eating is to be bored with life. This happens, but only to people whose unhappiness is very pronounced. The feast, small or large, is made to mark a special recurring moment or an unrepeatable occasion.

The bourgeois feast usually has more of a social than temporal significance. It is less a notch in time than the fulfilling of a social desideratum.

The feast for the peasant, when once the occasion has been given, begins with food and drink. It does so because food and drink have been reserved or put aside, on account of their rarity or special quality, for just such an occasion. Any feast, even if it is impromptu, has been partly prepared for for years. A feast is the consuming of the surplus saved and produced over and above daily needs. Expressing and using up some of this surplus, the feast is a double celebration – of the occasion which gives rise to it, and of the surplus itself. Hence its slow tempo, its generosity and the active high spirits which accompany it.

The feast for the bourgeois is an additional expense. What distinguishes its food from that of an ordinary meal is the amount of money spent. The true celebration of a surplus is beyond him, because he can never have a surplus of money.

The purpose of these comparisons is not to idealize the peasant. Peasant attitudes are mostly, in the strict sense of the word, *conservative*. At least until recently, the physical reality of the peasant's conservatism has hindered his understanding of the political realities of the modern world. These realities were originally a bourgeois creation. The bourgeois once had, and still to some degree retains, a mastery of the world of his own making.

I have tried to outline by using comparisons two modes of acquisition, of possessing, through the act of eating. If one examines each point of comparison, it becomes clear that the peasant way of eating is centred on the act of eating itself and on the food eaten: it is centripetal and physical. Whereas the bourgeois way of eating is centred on fantasy, ritual and spectacle: it is centrifugal and cultural. The first can complete itself in satisfaction; the second is never complete and gives rise to an appetite which, in essence, is insatiable.

1976

Field

'Life is not a walk across an open field' – Russian proverb

Shelf of a field, green, within easy reach, the grass on it not yet high, papered with blue sky through which yellow has grown to make pure green, the surface colour of what the basin of the world contains, attendant field, shelf between sky and sea, fronted with a curtain of printed trees, friable at its edges, the corners of it rounded, answering the sun with heat, shelf on a wall through which from time to time a cuckoo is audible, shelf on which she keeps the invisible and intangible jars of her pleasure, field that I have always known, I am lying raised up on one elbow wondering whether in any direction I can see beyond where you stop. The wire around you is the horizon.

Remember what it was like to be sung to sleep. If you are fortunate, the memory will be more recent than childhood. The repeated lines of words and music are like paths. These paths are circular and the rings they make are linked together like those of a chain. You walk along these paths and are led by them in circles which lead from one to the other, further and further away. The field upon which you walk and upon which the chain is laid is the song.

Into the silence, which was also at times a roar, of my thoughts and questions forever returning to myself to search there for an explanation of my life and its purpose, into this concentrated tiny hub of dense silent noise came the cackle of a hen from a nearby back garden, and at that moment that cackle, its distinct sharp-edged existence beneath a blue sky with white clouds, induced in me an intense awareness of freedom. The noise of the hen, which I could not even see, was an event (like a dog running or an artichoke flowering) in a field which until then had been awaiting a first event in order to become itself realizable. I knew that in that field I could listen to all sounds, all music.

From the city centre there are two ways back to the satellite city in which I live: the main road with a lot of traffic, and a side road which goes over a level crossing. The second is quicker unless you have to wait for a train at the crossing. During the spring and early summer I invariably take the side road, and I find myself hoping that the level crossing will be shut. In the angle between the railway lines and the road there is a field, surrounded on its other two sides by trees. The grass is tall in the field and in the evening when the sun is low, the green of the grass divides into light and dark grains of colour – as might happen to a bunch of parsley if lit up by the beam of a powerful lamp at night. Blackbirds hide in the grass and rise up from it. Their coming and going remains quite unaffected by the trains.

This field affords me considerable pleasure. Why then do I not sometimes walk there – it is quite near my flat – instead of relying on being stopped there by the closed level crossing? It is a question of contingencies overlapping. The events which take place in the field – two birds chasing one another, a cloud crossing the sun and changing the colour of the green – acquire a special significance because they occur during the minute or two during which I am obliged to wait. It is as though these minutes fill a certain area of time which exactly fits the spatial area of the field. Time and space conjoin.

The experience which I am attempting to describe by one tentative approach after another is very precise and is immediately recognizable. But it exists at a level of perception and feeling which is probably preverbal – hence, very much, the difficulty of writing about it.

Undoubtedly this experience must have a psychological history, beginning in infancy, which might be explained in psychoanalytic terms. But such explanations do not generalize the experience, they merely systematize it. The experience in one form or another is, I believe, a common one. It is seldom referred to only because it is nameless.

Let me now try to describe this experience diagrammatically in its ideal mode. What are the simplest things that can be said about it? The experience concerns a field. Not necessarily the same one. Any field, if perceived in a certain way, may offer it. But the *ideal* field, the field most likely to generate the experience, is:

1. A grass field. Why? It must be an area with boundaries which are visible – though not necessarily regular; it cannot be an unbounded segment of nature the limits to which are only set by the natural focus of your eyes. Yet within the area there should be a minimum of

order, a minimum of planned events. Neither crops nor regularly planted lines of fruit trees are ideal.

2. A field on a hillside, seen either from above like a table top, or from below when the incline of the hill appears to tilt the field towards you – like music on a music stand. Again, why? Because then the effects of perspective are reduced to a minimum and the relation between what is distant and near is a more equal one.

3. Not a field in winter. Winter is a season of inaction when the range of what is likely to happen is reduced.

4. A field which is not hedged on all sides: ideally, therefore, a continental rather than an English field. A completely hedged field with only a couple of gates leading into it limits the number of possible exits or entrances (except for birds).

Two things might be suggested by the above prescriptions. The ideal field would apparently have certain qualities in common with (a) a painting – defined edges, an accessible distance, and so on; and (b) a theatre-in-the-round stage – an attendant openness to events, with a maximum possibility for exits and entrances.

I believe, however, that suggestions like this are misleading, because they invoke a cultural context which, if it has anything whatsoever to do with the experience in question, can only refer *back* to it rather than precede it.

Given the ideal field now suggested, what are the further constitutive elements of the experience? It is here that the difficulties begin. You are before the field, although it seldom happens that your attention is drawn to the field before you have noticed an event within it.

Usually the event draws your attention to the field, and, almost instantaneously, your own awareness of the field then gives a special significance to the event.

The first event – since every event is part of a process – invariably leads to other, or, more precisely, invariably leads you to observe others in the field. The first event may be almost anything, provided that it is not in itself over-dramatic.

If you saw a man cry out and fall down, the implications of the event would immediately break the self-sufficiency of the field. You would run into it from the outside. You would try to take him out of it. Even if no physical action is demanded, any over-dramatic event will have the same disadvantage.

If you saw a tree being struck by lightning, the dramatic force of the event would inevitably lead you to interpret it in terms which at that moment would seem larger than the field before you. So, the first event should not be over-dramatic but otherwise it can be almost anything:

Two horses grazing.

A dog running in narrowing circles.

An old woman looking for mushrooms.

A hawk hovering above.

Finches chasing each other from bush to bush.

Chickens pottering.

Two men talking.

A flock of sheep moving exceedingly slowly from one corner to the centre.

A voice calling.

A child walking.

The first event leads you to notice further events which may be consequences of the first, or which may be entirely unconnected with it except that they take place in the same field. Often the first event which fixes your attention is more obvious than the subsequent ones. Having noticed the dog, you notice a butterfly. Having noticed the horses, you hear a woodpecker and then see it fly across a corner of the field. You watch a child walking and when he has left the field deserted and eventless, you notice a cat jump down into it from the top of a wall.

By this time you are within the experience. Yet saying this implies narrative time and the essence of the experience is that it takes place outside such time. The experience does not enter into the narrative of your life – that narrative which, at one level or another of your consciousness, you are continually retelling and developing to yourself. On the contrary, this narrative is interrupted. The visible extension of the field in space displaces awareness of your own lived time. By what precise mechanism does it do this?

You relate the events which you have seen and are still seeing to the field. It is not only that the field frames them, it also *contains* them. The existence of the field is the precondition for their occurring in the way that they have done and for the way in which others are still occurring. All events exist as definable events by virtue of their relation to other events. You have defined the events you have seen primarily (but not necessarily exclusively) by relating them to the event of the field, which at the same time is literally and symbolically the *ground* of the events which are taking place within it.

You may complain that I have now suddenly changed my use of the word 'event'. At first I referred to the field as a space awaiting events; now I refer to it as an event in itself. But this inconsistency parallels exactly the apparently illogical nature of the experience. Suddenly an experience of disinterested observation opens in its centre and gives birth to a happiness which is instantly recognizable as your own.

The field that you are standing before appears to have the same proportions as your own life.

1971

They Are the Last

for Beverly

Behind her tongue
with its language of grass
and passion for salt,
behind the heavy tongue
deft nevertheless
as a blind man's hand,
a cow in good health chews
approximately fifty times
before reswallowing the cud.

It appears the animals
Beverly
are emigrating: their America
the constellations in the sky
Lizard, Lion, Great Bear,
Ram, Bull, Crow,
Hare . . .
perhaps the more prudent
like the agouti
have chosen the milky way.

Put your ear to her flank
and you will hear
the tide of her four stomachs.
Her second, like a net,

has the name of a constellation:
Reticulum. Her third,
the Psalterium, is like
the pages of a book.

When she falls sick
and lacks the will to chew
her four stomachs fall
silent as a hive in winter.

Each year more animals depart.

Only pets and carcasses remain,
and the carcasses living or dead
are from birth
ineluctably and invisibly
turned into meat.
'I believe it's completely feasible,'
said Bob Rust
of Iowa State University,
'to specifically design
an animal for hamburger.'

Elsewhere
the animals of the poor
die with the poor
from protein insufficiency.

When fetched from the pastures
they bring into the cool stable
the heat of the orchard
and the hot breath of wild garlic.

To clean out the cowshed
scatter a little of
the mare's dung
it absorbs their shit
liquid as springtime
and green with grass.
And fasten them well tonight
bed them with beech leaves
Beverly
they are the last.

Now that they have gone
it is their endurance we miss.
Unlike the tree
the river or the cloud
the animals had eyes
and in their glance
was permanence.

It was the same fox for ever and ever.
To kill him
was to drag him
momentarily
from the earth
of his eternity.

Once flies and crows
when devouring the dead sheep
began with the eyes.
Yet the ewe
had already lambed
her permanence.

They Are the Last

The buzzard circled
biding his everlasting time
as repeatedly
as the mountain.

Out of the single night
came the day's look,
the wary animal glance
on every side.

Once the animals flowed like their milk.

Now that they have gone
it is their endurance we miss.

*

'The breeding sow,' it is said,

'should be thought of and treated
as a valuable piece of machinery
whose function
is to pump out baby pigs.'

*

Sometimes still,
when you are pouring
from the white jug,
the milk
reminds me of the geese
who like dogs
guarded the house.

2001

Ernst Fischer: A Philosopher and Death

It was the last day of his life. Of course we did not know it then – not until almost ten o'clock in the evening. Three of us spent the day with him: Lou (his wife), Anya and myself. I can write now only of my own experience of that day. If I tried to write about theirs – much as I was conscious of it at the time and later – I would nevertheless run the risk of writing fiction.

Ernst Fischer was in the habit of spending the summer in a small village in Styria. He and Lou stayed in the house of three sisters who were old friends and who had been Austrian Communists with Ernst and his two brothers in the 1930s. The youngest of the three sisters, who now runs the house, was imprisoned by the Nazis for hiding and aiding political refugees. The man with whom she was then in love was beheaded for a similar political offence.

It is necessary to describe this in order not to give a false impression of the garden which surrounds their house. The garden is full of flowers, large trees, grass banks and a lawn. A stream flows through it, conducted through a wooden pipe the diameter of an immense barrel. It runs the length of the garden, then across fields to a small dynamo which belongs to a neighbour. Everywhere in the garden there is the sound of water, gentle but persistent. There are two small fountains: tiny pin-like jets of water force their way hissing through holes in the wooden barrel-line; water flows into and empties continually from a nineteenth-century swimming pool (built by the grandfather of the three sisters): in this pool, now surrounded by tall grass, and itself green, trout swim and occasionally jump splashing to the surface.

It often rains in Styria, and if you are in this house you sometimes have the impression that it is still raining after it has stopped on account of the sound of water in the garden. Yet the garden is not damp and many colours of many flowers break up its greenness. The garden is a kind of sanctuary. But to grasp its full meaning one must, as I said, remember that in its outhouses men and women were hiding for their lives thirty years ago and were protected by the three sisters who now arrange vases of flowers and let rooms to a few old friends in the summer in order to make ends meet.

When I arrived in the morning Ernst was walking in the garden. He was thin and upright. And he trod very lightly, as though his weight, such as it was, was never fully planted on the ground. He wore a wide-brimmed white-and-grey hat which Lou had recently bought for him. He wore the hat like he wore all his clothes, lightly, elegantly, but without concern. He was fastidious – not about details of dress, but about the nature of appearances.

The gate to the garden was difficult to open and shut, but he had mastered it and so, as usual, he fastened it behind me. The previous day Lou had felt somewhat unwell. I enquired how she was. 'She is better,' he said, 'you have only to look at her!' He said this with youthful, unrestricted pleasure. He was seventy-three years old and when he was dying the doctor, who did not know him, said he looked older, but he had none of the muted expressions of the old. He took present pleasures at their full face-value and his capacity to do this was in no way diminished by political disappointment or by the bad news which since 1968 had persistently arrived from so many places. He was a man without a trace, without a line on his face, of bitterness. Some, I suppose, might therefore call him an innocent. They would be wrong. He was a man who refused to jettison or diminish his very high quotient of belief. Instead he readjusted its objects and their relative order. Recently he *believed* in scepticism. He even believed in the necessity of apocalyptic visions in the hope that they would act as warnings.

It is the surety and strength of his convictions which now make it seem that he died so suddenly. His health had been frail since childhood. He was often ill. Recently his eyesight had begun to fail and he could read only with a powerful magnifying glass – more often Lou read to him. Yet despite this it was quite impossible for anyone who knew him to suppose that he was dying slowly, that every year he belonged a little less vehemently to life. He was fully alive because he was fully convinced.

What was he convinced of? His books, his political interventions, his speeches are there on record to answer the question. Or do they not answer it fully enough? He was convinced that capitalism would eventually destroy man – or be overthrown. He had no illusions about the ruthlessness of the ruling class everywhere. He recognized that we lacked a model for Socialism. He was impressed by and highly interested in what is happening in China, but he did not believe in a Chinese model. What is so hard, he said, is that we are forced back to offering visions.

We walked towards the end of the garden, where there is a small lawn surrounded by bushes and a willow tree. He used to lie there talking with animated gestures, fingers plucking, hands turning out and drawing in – as though literally winding the wool from off his listeners' eyes. As he talked, his shoulders bent forward to follow his hands; as he listened, his head inclined forward to follow the speaker's words. (He knew the exact angle at which to adjust the back of his deckchair.)

Now the same lawn, the deckchairs piled in the outhouse, appears oppressively, flagrantly empty. It is far harder to walk across it without a shiver than it was to turn down the sheet and look again and again at his face. The Russian believers say that the spirits of the departed stay in their familiar surroundings for forty days. Perhaps this is based on a fairly accurate observation of the stages of mourning. At any rate it is hard for me to believe that if a total stranger wandered into the garden now, he would not notice that the end under the willow tree surrounded by bushes was flagrantly empty, like a deserted house on the point of becoming a ruin. Its emptiness is palpable. And yet it is not.

It had already begun to rain and so we went to sit in his room for a while before going out to lunch. We used to sit, the four of us, round a small round table, talking. Sometimes I faced the window and looked out at the trees and the forests on the hills. That morning I pointed out that when the frame with the mosquito net was fitted over the window, everything looked more or less two-dimensional and so composed itself. We give too much weight to space, I went on – there's perhaps more of nature in a Persian carpet than in most landscape paintings. 'We'll take the hills down, push the trees aside and hang up carpets for you,' said Ernst. 'Your other trousers,' remarked Lou, 'why don't you put them on as we're going out?' Whilst he changed we went on talking. 'There,' he said, smiling ironically at the task he had just performed, 'is that better now?' 'They are very elegant, but they are the same pair!' I said. He laughed, delighted at this remark. Delighted because it emphasized that he had changed his trousers only to satisfy Lou's whim, and that that was reason enough for him; delighted because an insignificant difference was treated as though it didn't exist; delighted because, encapsulated in a tiny joke, there was a tiny conspiracy against the existent.

The Etruscans buried their dead in chambers under the ground and on the walls they painted scenes of pleasure and everyday life such as the dead had known. To have the light to see what they were painting they made a small hole in the ground above and then used mirrors to reflect the sunlight onto the particular image on which they were working. With words I try to decorate, as though it were a tomb, the last day of his life.

We were going to have lunch in a *pension* high up in

the forests and hills. The idea was to look and see whether it would be suitable for Ernst to work there during September or October. Earlier in the year Lou had written to dozens of small hotels and boarding houses and this was the only one which was cheap and sounded promising. They wanted to take advantage of my having a car to go and have a look.

There are no scandals to make. But there is a contrast to draw. Two days after his death there was a long article about him in *Le Monde*. 'Little by little,' it wrote, 'Ernst Fischer has established himself as one of the most original and rewarding thinkers of "heretical" Marxism.' He had influenced an entire generation of the left in Austria. During the last four years he was continually denounced in Eastern Europe for the significant influence he had had on the thinking of the Czechs who had created the Prague Spring. His books were translated into most languages. But the conditions of his life during the last five years were cramped and harsh. The Fischers had little money, were always subject to financial worries, and lived in a small, noisy workers' flat in Vienna. Why not? I hear his opponents ask. Was he better than the workers? No, but he needed professional working conditions. In any case he himself did not complain. But with the unceasing noise of families and radios in the flats above and on each side he found it impossible to work as concentratedly in Vienna as he wished to do and was capable of doing. Hence the annual search for quiet, cheap places in the country – where three months might represent so many chapters completed. The three sisters' house was not available after August.

We drove up a steep dust road through the forest. Once I asked a child the way in my terrible German and the child did not understand and simply stuffed her fist into her mouth in amazement. The others laughed at me. It was raining lightly: the trees were absolutely still. And I remember thinking as I drove round the hairpin bends that if I could define or realize the nature of the submission of the trees, I would learn something about the human body too – at least about the human body when loved. The rain ran down the trees. A leaf is so easily moved. A breath of wind is sufficient. And yet not a leaf moved.

We found the *pension*. The young woman and her husband were expecting us and they showed us to a long table where some other guests were already eating. The room was large with a bare wooden floor and big windows from which you looked over the shoulders of some nearby steep fields across the forest to the plain below. It was not unlike a canteen in a youth hostel, except that there were cushions on the benches and flowers on the tables. The food was simple but good. After the meal we were to be shown the rooms. The husband came over with an architect's plan in his hands. 'By next year everything will be different,' he explained; 'the owners want to make more money and so they're going to convert the rooms and put bathrooms in and put up their prices. But this autumn you can still have the two rooms on the top floor as they are, and there'll be nobody else up there, you'll be quiet.'

We climbed to the rooms. They were identical, side by side, with the lavatory on the same landing opposite them. Each room was narrow, with a bed against the wall, a wash-basin and an austere cupboard, and at the end of it a window with a view of miles and miles of landscape. 'You can put a table in front of the window and work here.' 'Yes, yes,' he said. 'You'll finish the book.' 'Perhaps not all of it, but I could get much done.' 'You must take it,' I said. I visualized him sitting at the table in front of the window, looking down at the still trees. The book was the second volume of his auto-biography. It covered the period 1945–55 – when he had been very active in Austrian and international politics – and it was to deal principally with the development and consequences of the Cold War which he saw, I think, as the counter-revolutionary reaction, on both sides of what was to become the Iron Curtain, to the popular victories of 1945. I visualized his magnifying glass on the small table, his note-pad, the pile of current reference books, the chair pushed away when, stiffly but light on his feet, he had gone downstairs to take his regular walk before lunch. 'You must take it,' I said again.

We went for a walk together, the walk into the forest he would take each morning. I asked him why in the first volume of his memoirs he wrote in several distinctly different styles.

'Each style belongs to a different person.'

'To a different aspect of yourself?'

'No, rather it belongs to a different self.'

'Do these different selves coexist, or, when one is predominant, are the others absent?'

'They are present together at the same time. None can disappear. The two strongest are my violent, hot, extremist, romantic self and the other my distant, sceptical self.'

'Do they discourse together in your head?'

'No.' (He had a special way of saying No. As if he had long ago considered the question at length and after much patient investigation had arrived at the answer.)

'They watch each other,' he continued. 'The sculptor Hrdlicka has done a head of me in marble. It makes me look much younger than I am. But you can see these two predominant selves in me – each corresponding to a side of my face. One is perhaps a little like Danton, the other a little like Voltaire.'

As we walked along the forest path, I changed sides so as to examine his face, first from the right and then from the left. Each eye was different and was confirmed in its difference by the corner of the mouth on each side of his face. The right side was tender and wild. He had mentioned Danton. I thought rather of an animal: perhaps a kind of goat, light on its feet, a chamois maybe. The left side was sceptical but harsher: it made judgements but kept them to itself, it appealed to reason with an unswerving certainty. The left side would have been inflexible had it not been compelled to live with the right. I changed sides again to check my observations.

'And have their relative strengths always been the same?' I asked.

'The sceptical self has become stronger,' he said. 'But there are other selves too.' He smiled at me and took my arm and added, as though to reassure me: 'Its hegemony is not complete!'

He said this a little breathlessly and in a slightly deeper

voice than usual – in the voice in which he spoke when moved, for example when embracing a person he loved.

His walk was very characteristic. His hips moved stiffly, but otherwise he walked like a young man, quickly, lightly, to the rhythm of his own reflections. 'The present book,' he said, 'is written in a consistent style – detached, reasoning, cool.'

'Because it comes later?'

'No, because it is not really about myself. It is about an historical period. The first volume is also about myself and I could not have told the truth if I had written it all in the same voice. There was no self which was above the struggle of the others and could have told the story evenly. The categories we make between different aspects of experience – so that, for instance, some people say I should not have spoken about love *and* about the Comintern in the same book – these categories are mostly there for the convenience of liars.'

'Does one self hide its decisions from the others?'

Maybe he didn't hear the question. Maybe he wanted to say what he said whatever the question.

'My first decision,' he said, 'was not to die. I decided when I was a child, in a sick-bed, with death at hand, that I wanted to live.'

From the *pension* we drove down to Graz. Lou and Anya needed to do some shopping; Ernst and I installed ourselves in the lounge of an old hotel by the river. It was in this hotel that I had come to see Ernst on my way to Prague in the summer of '68. He had given me addresses, advice, information, and summarized for me the historical background to the new events taking place. Our interpretation of these events was not exactly the same, but it seems pointless now to try to define our small differences. Not because Ernst is dead, but because those events were buried alive and we see only their large contours heaped beneath the earth. Our specific points of difference no longer exist because the choices to which they applied no longer exist. Nor will they ever exist again in quite the same way. Opportunities can be irretrievably lost and then their loss is like a death. When the Russian tanks entered Prague in August 1968 Ernst was absolutely lucid about that death.

In the lounge of the hotel I remembered the occasion of four years before. He had already been worried. Unlike many Czechs, he considered it quite likely that Brezhnev would order the Red Army to move in. But he still hoped. And this hope still carried within it all the other hopes which had been born in Prague that spring.

After 1968 Ernst began to concentrate his thoughts on the past. But he remained incorrigibly orientated towards the future. His view of the past was for the benefit of the future – for the benefit of the great or terrible transformations it held in store. But after '68 he recognized that the path towards any revolutionary transformation was bound to be long and tortuous and that Socialism in Europe would be deferred beyond his lifespan. Hence the best use of his remaining time was to bear witness to the past.

We did not talk about this in the hotel, for there was nothing new to decide. The important thing was to finish the second volume of his memoirs and that very morning we had found a way of making this happen more quickly. Instead, we talked of love: or, more exactly, about the state of being in love. Our talk followed roughly these lines.

The capacity to fall in love is now thought of as natural and universal – and as a passive capacity. (Love strikes. Love-struck.) Yet there have been whole periods when the possibility of falling in love did not exist. Being in love in fact depends upon the possibility of free active choice – or anyway an apparent possibility. What does the lover choose? He chooses to stake the world (the whole of his life) against the beloved. The beloved concentrates all the possibilities of the world within her and thus offers the realization of all his own potentialities. The beloved for the lover empties the world of hope (the world that does not include her). Strictly speaking, being in love is a mood in so far as it is infinitely extensive – it reaches beyond the stars; but it cannot develop without changing its nature, and so it cannot endure.

The equivalence between the beloved and the world is confirmed by sex. To make love with the beloved is, subjectively, to possess and be possessed by the world. Ideally, what remains outside the experience is – nothing. Death of course is within it.

This provokes the imagination to its very depths. One wants to use the world in the act of love. One wants to make love with fish, with fruit, with hills, with forests, in the sea.

And those, said Ernst, 'are the metamorphoses! It is nearly always that way round in Ovid. The beloved becomes a tree, a stream, a hill. Ovid's *Metamorphoses* are not poetic conceits, they are really about the relation between the world and the poet in love.'

I looked into his eyes. They were pale. (Invariably they were moist with the strain of seeing.) They were pale like some blue flower bleached to a whitish grey by the sun. Yet despite their moisture and their paleness, the light which had bleached them was still reflected in them.

'The passion of my life,' he said, 'was Lou. I had many love affairs. Some of them, when I was a student here in Graz, in this hotel. I was married. With all the other women I loved there was a debate, a discourse about our different interests. With Lou there is no discourse because our interests are the same. I don't mean we never argue. She argued for Trotsky when I was still a Stalinist. But our interest – below all our interests – is singular. When I first met her, I said No. I remember the evening very well. I knew immediately I saw her, and I said No to myself. I knew that if I had a love affair with her, everything would stop. I would never love another woman. I would live monogamously. I thought I would not be able to work. We would do nothing except make love over and over again. The world would never be the same. She knew too. Before going home to Berlin she asked me very calmly: "Do you want me to stay?" "No," I said.'

Lou came back from the shops with some cheeses and yoghurts she had bought.

'Today we have talked for hours about me,' said Ernst, 'you don't talk about yourself. Tomorrow we shall talk about you.'

On the way out of Graz I stopped at a bookshop to find Ernst a copy of some poems by the Serbian poet Miodrag Pavlovic. Ernst had said sometime during the afternoon that he no longer wrote poems and no longer saw the purpose of poetry. 'It may be,' he added, 'that my idea of poetry is outdated.' I wanted him to read Pavlovic's poems. I gave him the book in the car. 'I already have it,' he said. But he put his hand on my shoulders. For the last time without suffering.

We were going to have supper in the café in the village. On the stairs outside his room, Ernst, who was behind me, suddenly but softly cried out. I turned round immediately. He had both his hands pressed to the small of his back. 'Sit down,' I said, 'lie down.' He took no notice. He was looking past me into the distance. His attention was there, not here. At the time I thought this was because the pain was bad. But it seemed to pass quite quickly. He descended the stairs – no more slowly than usual. The three sisters were waiting at the front door to wish us good night. We stopped a moment to talk. Ernst explained that his rheumatism had jabbed him in the back.

There was a curious distance about him. Either he consciously suspected what had happened, or else the chamois in him, the animal that was so strong in him, had already left to look for a secluded place in which to die. I question whether I am now using hindsight. I am not. He was already distant.

We walked, chatting, through the garden past the sounds of water. Ernst opened the gate and fastened it because it was difficult, for the last time.

We sat at our usual table in the public bar of the café. Some people were having their evening drink. They went out. The landlord, a man only interested in stalking and shooting deer, switched off two of the lights and went out to fetch our soup. Lou was furious and shouted after him. He didn't hear. She got up, went behind the bar and switched on the two lights again. 'I would have done the same,' I said. Ernst smiled at Lou and then at Anya and me. 'If you and Lou lived together,' he said, 'it would be explosive.'

When the next course came Ernst was unable to eat it. The landlord came up to enquire whether it was not good. 'It is excellently prepared,' said Ernst, holding up the untouched plate of food in front of him, 'and excellently cooked, but I am afraid that I cannot eat it.'

He looked pale and he said he had pains in the lower part of his stomach.

'Let us go back,' I said. Again he appeared – in response to the suggestion – to look into the distance. 'Not yet,' he said, 'in a little while.'

We finished eating. He was unsteady on his feet but he insisted on standing alone. On the way to the door he placed his hand on my shoulder – as he had in the car. But it expressed something very different. And the touch of his hand was now even lighter.

After we had driven a few hundred metres he said: 'I think I may be going to faint.' I stopped and put my arm round him. His head fell on my shoulder. He was breathing in short gasps. With his left, sceptical eye he looked hard up into my face. A sceptical, questioning, unswerving look. Then his look became unseeing. The light which had bleached his eyes was no longer in them. He was breathing heavily.

Anya flagged down a passing car and went back to the village to fetch help. She came back in another car. When she opened the door of our car, Ernst tried to move his feet out. It was his last instinctive movement – to be ordered, willed, neat.

When we reached the house, the news had preceded us and the gates, which were difficult, were already open so that we could drive up to the front door. The young man who had brought Anya from the village carried Ernst indoors and upstairs over his shoulders. I walked behind to stop his head banging against the door-jambs. We laid him down on his bed. We did helpless things to occupy ourselves whilst waiting for the doctor. But even waiting for the doctor was a pretext. There was nothing to do. We massaged his feet, we fetched a hot-water bottle, we felt his pulse. I stroked his cold head. His brown hands on the white sheet, curled up but not grasping, looked quite separate from the rest of the body. They appeared cut off by his cuffs. Like the forefeet cut off from an animal found dead in the forest.

The doctor arrived. A man of fifty. Tired, pale-faced, sweating. He wore a peasant's suit without a tie. He was like a veterinary surgeon. 'Hold his arm,' he said, 'whilst I give this injection.' He inserted the needle finely in the vein so that the liquid should flow along it like the water along the barrel-pipe in the garden. At this moment we were alone in the room together. The doctor shook his head. 'How old is he?' 'Seventy-three.' 'He looks older,' he said.

'He looked younger when he was alive,' I said.

'Has he had an infarctus before?'

'Yes.'

'He has no chance this time,' he said.

Lou, Anya, the three sisters and I stood around his bed. He had gone.

Besides painting scenes from everyday life on the walls of their tombs, the Etruscans carved on the lids of their sarcophagi full-length figures representing the dead. Usually these figures are half-reclining, raised on one elbow, feet and legs relaxed as though on a couch, but head and neck alert as they gaze into the distance. Many thousands of such carvings were executed quickly and more or less according to a formula. But however stereotyped the rest of these figures, their alertness as they look into the distance is striking. Given the context, the distance is surely a temporal rather than a spatial one: the distance is the future the dead projected when alive. They look into that distance as though they could stretch out a hand and touch it.

I can make no sarcophagus carving. But there are pages written by Ernst Fischer where it seems to me that the writer wrote adopting an equivalent stance, achieving a similar quality of expectation.

1974

THE STORY OF PENGUIN CLASSICS

Before 1946 ...'Classics' are mainly the domain of academics and students, without readable editions for everyone else. This all changes when a little-known classicist, E. V. Rieu, presents Penguin founder Allen Lane with the translation of Homer's Odyssey that he has been working on and reading to his wife Nelly in his spare time.

1946 The Odyssey becomes the first Penguin Classic published, and promptly sells three million copies. Suddenly, classic books are no longer for the privileged few.

1950s Rieu, now series editor, turns to professional writers for the best modern, readable translations, including Dorothy L. Sayers's *Inferno* and Robert Graves's *The Twelve Caesars*, which revives the salacious original.

1960s 1961 sees the arrival of the Penguin Modern Classics, showcasing the best twentieth-century writers from around the world. Rieu retires in 1964, hailing the Penguin Classics list as 'the greatest educative force of the 20th century'.

1970s A new generation of translators arrives to swell the Penguin Classics ranks, and the list grows to encompass more philosophy, religion, science, history and politics.

1980s The Penguin American Library joins the Classics stable, with titles such as *The Last of the Mohicans* safeguarded. Penguin Classics now offers the most comprehensive library of world literature available.

1990s Penguin Popular Classics are launched, offering readers budget editions of the greatest works of literature. Penguin Audiobooks brings the classics to a listening audience for the first time, and in 1999 the launch of the Penguin Classics website takes them online to an ever larger global readership.

The 21st Century Penguin Classics are rejacketed for the first time in nearly twenty years. This world famous series now consists of more than 1,300 titles, making the widest range of the best books ever written available to millions – and constantly redefining the meaning of what makes a 'classic'.

The Odyssey continues ...

The best books ever written

PENGUIN ● CLASSICS

SINCE 1946